'FOOD SAFETY AND STANDARD ACT 2006' - SUPREME COURT AND HIGH COURT'S LEADING CASE LAWS

CASE NOTES- FACTS- FINDINGS OF APEX COURT JUDGES & CITATIONS

JAYPRAKASH BANSILAL SOMANI

Made with ♥ on the Notion Press Platform
www.notionpress.com

All the Past & Present Judges of the Supreme Court of India.

Salute to their wisdom.

Salute to their interpretation of Law.

Salute to their elaborative judgement writing.

Supreme Court Of India

Contents

Contents

Preface

Dear Learned Advocates ofTrial Court, High court and Supreme Court, Corporate and Individuals.

I am very delighted to provide you a book on 'FOOD SAFETY AND STANDARD ACT 2006'- SUPREME COURT'S LATEST LEADING CASE LAWs.

In this book you will get...

1. Name of the Case i. e. Cause title

2.Relevant Sections discussed in the case

3. Hon'ble Judges/Coram of the case

4.Number of PDF Pages in Original Judgement of the case

5. All available Citations of the case

6. Case Note with appeal allowed/ dismissed or disposed off

7. Facts of the case

8. Hon'ble Apex Court's findings, while dismissing/allowing or disposing the appeal

9. Ratio Decidendi if any.

My special thanks to Manupatra, because of their web portal I can compile this book in well manner. I am also thankful to Notion Press to support me to publish & market this book throughout the Country. Thanks to my Juniors, Advocate Colleagues & Insolvency Professional Colleagues to support me in this venture.

Adv. Manoj Kumar Chowdhary & Miss. Arvind Pooja Rai has helped me a lot to compile this book. I hope this book will add some value addition in the wealth of your legal knowledge. Your positive feedbacks will boost me to compile/ write further books & negative feedbacks will improve my skills. Kindly send your valuable feedbacks by email.

Thanks with Regards,

Jayprakash B. Somani

Advocate, Supreme Court of India

Email: jaysomani64@gmail.com

Web Site:www.jayprakashsomani.com

Call: 9322188701, 8459194576

Acknowledgements

Printed & Published by
Notion Press
No. 8, 3rd Cross Street,
CIT Colony, Mylapore,
Chennai, Tamil Nadu- 600004
Managed by
Jayprakash Somani Advocates & Solicitors
Law Firm for Supreme Court of India
Delhi Office
B- 851, 1st Floor, Shivaji Marg, New Ashok Nagar, Delhi 110096.
Call: 9322188701, 8459194576
Supreme Court Chamber
312, 3rd Floor, M. C. Setalvad Block, In front of 'D' Gate, Bhagwan Das
Road, Supreme Court of India, New Delhi 110001
Contact: 8459194576, 9811011747
www.jayprakashsomani.com
Download our app to get access to our Free Videos, Free Bare Acts,
Free Study Material in Legal as well as International Business Regime.
Android App Link ;-https://clpandrea.page.link/cmSm
Ios APp Link :-https://apps.apple.com/us/app/classplus/id1324522260
Login with org code ;- (qywzji)
Web Link ;-https://qywzji.courses.store/
Opportunity for Lawyers/ Social Workers to get Supreme Court Law
Firm JSAS's authorised centre at District Level.
Kindly Message or Call to: 9322188701
Books are available online in India
1.**Notion Press:**https://notionpress.com/author/jayprakash_somani
2.**Amazon:**https://www.amazon.in/s?k=jayprakash+somani
3.**Flipkart:**https://www.flipkart.com/search?q=Jayprakash%20Somani
Books are available online at International Market
4. **Amazon International:** https://www.amazon.com/
s?k=jayprakash+somani
5. **Amazon United Kingdom:** https://www.amazon.co.uk/
s?k=jayprakash+somani

6. **E-Books/Kindle edition at National & International Level:** https://www.amazon.in/s?k=jaypraksh+somani

Securities and Exchange Board of India and Ors. vs. Kanaiyalal Baldevbhai Patel and Ors. (20.09.2017 - SC) : MANU/SC/1188/2017

Relative Section:

Securities and Exchange Board of India Act, 1992 - Section 12, Section 12A, Section 15HA, Section 30;

Indian Contract Act, 1872;

Monopolies and Restrictive Trade Practices Act, 1969 [Repealed] - Section 36A;

Consumer Protection Act, 1986 - Section 2(1);

Competition Act, 2002 - Section 3;

Food Safety and Standards Act, 2006 - Section 24(2);

Specific Relief Act 1963 - Section 20;

Usurious Loans Act, 1918 - Section 3;

Securities and Exchange Board of India (Prohibition of Fraudulent and Unfair Trade Practices relating to Securities Market) Regulations, 1995; Securities and Exchange Board of India (Prohibition of Fraudulent and Unfair Trade Practices relating to the Securities Market) Regulations, 2003 - Regulation 1,Regulation 2, Regulation 2(1),) Regulation 2(3), Regulation 2(4), Regulation 3, Regulation 4, Regulation 4(1), Regulation 4(2), Regulation 5; Securities and Exchange Board of India (Prohibition of

Fraudulent and Unfair Trade Practices Relating to Securities Market) (Amendment) Regulations, 2013;

Securities Exchange Act, 1934 - Section 10

Hon'bleJudges/Coram:

Ranjan Gogoi and N.V. Ramana, JJ.

Equivalent Citation: IV(2017)BC643(SC), [2017]141CLA254(SC), [2018]207CompCas416(SC), (2017)4 CompLJ401(SC), 2017/INSC/962, 2017/INSC/963, 2017/INSC/964, 2017/INSC/965, 2017/INSC/966, 2017(4) RCR(Civil)660, (11)SCALE600, (2017)15SCC1, 2017 (8) SCJ 650, [2017]144SCL5(SC), [2017]14SCR268

Case Reference:

Govind Impex Pvt. Ltd. v. Income Tax Department MANU/SC/1032/ 2010 : (2011) 1 SCC 529;Krishi Utpadan Mandi Samiti v. Pilibhit Pantnagar Beej Ltd. MANU/SC/0989/2003 : (2004) 1 SCC 391;Securities and Exchange Board of India v. Kishore R. Ajmera MANU/SC/0212/2016 : (2016) 6 SCC 368; N. Narayanan v. adjudicating Officer, SEBI MANU/SC/ 0426/2013 : (2013) 12 SCC 152; David Carpenter, Kenneth P. Felis and R. Foster Winans, v. United States MANU/USSC/0103/1987 : 484 U.S. 19;Hammerschmidt v.United States MANU/USSC/0081/1924: 265 U.S. 182 : 44 S. Ct. 511 : 68 L. Ed. 968 (1924);Grin v. Shine MANU /USSC / 0186/1902 : 187 U.S. 181 : 23 S. Ct. 98 : 47 L. Ed. 130 (1902); Snepp v. United States MANU / USSC /0146 /1980:444 U.S. 507 : 100 S. Ct. 763 : 62 L. Ed.2d 704 (1980);Diamond v. Oreamuno 24 N.Y.2d 494 : 301 N. Y.S.2d 78 : 248 N.E.2d 910 (1969); Vincent F. Chiarella v. United States MANU/ USSC/0117/1980 : 445 U.S. 222 (1980); Colquhoun v. Brooks (1887) 19 Q.B.D. 400; Lowe v. Darling & Sons (1906) 2 K.B. 772; Securities and Exchange Commission v. National Securities, Inc., et al MANU/USSC/ 0169/1969 : 393 U.S. 453 (1969)

NumberofPagesintheOriginalJudgment: 20

Case Note:

Capital Market - Imposition of penalty - Prohibition of Fraudulent and Unfair Trade Practices relating to Securities Market) Regulations, 2003 - Adjudicating Authorities imposed penalty on Respondents - Securities Appellate Tribunal before whom appeals were filed by Respondents interfered with orders passed by Adjudicating Authority primarily on ground that on reading of Regulation 2(c),(3) and Regulation (4) of Regulations it did not transpire that acts attributable amount to fraudulent or unfair trade practice warranting findings recorded by Adjudicating

Authority and imposition of penalty in question on that basis - Hence, present appeal - Whether front running by non-intermediary was prohibited practice under Regulations 3 (a), (b), (c) and (d) and 4(1) of Regulations.

Facts:

The Securities Appellate Tribunal before whom appeals were filed by the Respondents interfered with the orders passed by the Adjudicating Authority primarily on the ground that on a reading of Regulation 2(c),(3) and Regulation (4) of the Regulations it did not transpire that the acts attributable amount to fraudulent or unfair trade practice warranting the findings recorded by the Adjudicating Authority and the imposition of penalty in question on that basis. Hence, present appeal.

Held, while allowing the appeal:

N.V. Ramana, J.

(i) The law of confidentiality had a bearing on this case instant. Confidential information acquired or compiled by a corporation in the course and conduct of its business was a species of property to which the corporation has the exclusive right and benefit, and which a Court of equity will protect through the injunctive process or other appropriate remedy. The information of possible trades that the company was going to undertake is the confidential information of the company concerned, which it has absolute liberty to deal with. Therefore, a person conveying confidential information to another person (tippee) breaches his duty prescribed by law and if the recipient of such information knows of the breach and trades, and there was an inducement to bring about an inequitable result, then the recipient tippee may be said to have committed the fraud. [42]

(ii) Accordingly, non-intermediary front running may be brought under the prohibition prescribed under Regulations 3 and 4 (1), for being fraudulent or unfair trade practice, provided that the ingredients under those heads were satisfied. It was clear that in order to establish charges against tippee, Under Regulations 3 (a), (b), (c) and (d) and 4 (1) of FUTP 2003, one needs to prove that a person who had provided the tip was under a duty to keep the non-public information under confidence, further such breach of duty was known to the tippee and he still trades thereby defrauding the person, whose orders were front-runned, by inducing him to deal at the price he did. [43]

Ranjan Gogoi, J.: Concurring view

(iii) To attract the rigor of Regulations 3 and 4 of the 2003 Regulations, mensrea was not an indispensable requirement and the correct test is one of preponderance of probabilities. Merely because the operation of the aforesaid two provisions of the 2003 Regulations invite penal consequences on the defaulters, proof beyond reasonable doubt as held by present Court in Securities and Exchange Board of India v. Kishore R. Ajmera was not an indispensable requirement. The inferential conclusion from the proved and admitted facts, so long the same were reasonable and could be legitimately arrived at on a consideration of the totality of the materials, would be permissible and legally justified. Having regard to the facts of the present cases i.e. the volume of shares sold and purchased; the proximity of time between the transactions of sale and purchase and the repeated nature of transactions on different dates, the conduct of the Respondents were in breach of the code of business integrity in the securities market. The consequences for such breach including penal consequences. Orders passed by the Appellate Tribunal were set aside and the findings recorded and the penalty imposed by the Adjudicating Officer were restored. [58]

CHAPTER TWO

Mohd. Mustafa and Ors. vs. Union of India and Ors. (12.05.2017 – ALLHC) : MANU/UP/2324/2017

Relative Section:

Constitution Of India - Article 19, Constitution Of India - Article 21, Constitution Of India - Article 48, Constitution Of India - Article 51-A (g), Food Safety And Standards Act, 2006 - Section 3 (1) (zb), Food Safety And Standards Act, 2006 - Section 89, Food Safety And Standards Act, 2006 - Section 97 (2), Food Safety And Standards Act, 2006 - Section 97(2); General Clauses Act 1897 - Section 6; Prevention Of Cruelty To Animals Act, 1960 - Section 2 (e); Uttar Pradesh Kshettra Panchayats And Zila Panchayats Adhiniyam, 1961 - Section 197, Uttar Pradesh Kshettra Panchayats And Zila Panchayats Adhiniyam, 1961 - Section 198, Uttar Pradesh Kshettra Panchayats And Zila Panchayats Adhiniyam, 1961 - Section 229, Uttar Pradesh Kshettra Panchayats And Zila Panchayats Adhiniyam, 1961 - Section 230, Uttar Pradesh KshettraPanchayats And Zila Panchayats Adhiniyam, 1961 - Section 237, Uttar Pradesh Kshettra Panchayats And Zila Panchayats Adhiniyam, 1961 - Section 238, Uttar Pradesh Kshettra Panchayats And Zila Panchayats Adhiniyam, 1961 - Section 241; Uttar Pradesh MunicipalCorporations Act, 1959 - Section 114 (xxi), Uttar Pradesh Municipal Corporations Act, 1959 - Section 114(xx), Uttar Pradesh Municipal Corporations Act,1959 - Section 241, Uttar Pradesh Municipal Corporations Act, 1959 - Section 298 (2), Uttar Pradesh Municipal Corporations Act, 1959 - Section 421, Uttar Pradesh Municipal

Corporations Act, 1959 - Section 422, Uttar Pradesh Municipal Corporations Act, 1959 - Section 423, Uttar Pradesh Municipal Corporations Act, 1959 - Section 430, Uttar Pradesh Municipal Corporations Act, 1959 - Section 431, Uttar Pradesh Municipal Corporations Act, 1959 - Section 439, Uttar Pradesh Municipal Corporations Act, 1959 - Section 533; Uttar Pradesh Municipalities Act, 1916 - Section 35, Uttar Pradesh Municipalities Act, 1916 - Section 36, Uttar Pradesh Municipalities Act, 1916 - Section 7 (1) (h), Uttar Pradesh Municipalities Act, 1916 - Section 7(1)(h); Uttar Pradesh Revenue Code, 2006 - Section 97 (2); Water (prevention And Control Of Pollution) Act, 1974 - Section 33A

Hon'bleJudges/Coram:

Amreshwar Pratap Sahi and Sanjay Harkauli, JJ.

Equivalent Citation: 2017(5) ALJ 275

Case Reference:

Laxmi Narain Modi vs. Union of India (UOI) and Ors. MANU/SC/0782/2012; Laxmi Narain Modi vs. Union of India (UOI) and Ors. MANU/SC/0998/2013; Hinsa Virodhak Sangh vs. Mirzapur Moti Kuresh Jamat and Ors. MANU/SC/1246/2008; Mohd. Hanif Quareshi and Ors. vs. The State of Bihar MANU/SC/0027/1958; Abdul Hakim Quraishi and Ors. vs. The State of Bihar MANU/SC/0038/1960; Mohammed Faruk vs. State of Madhya Pradesh and Ors. MANU/SC/0046/1969; Hasmattullah vs. State of Madhya Pradesh and others MANU/SC/0518/1996; Om Prakash and Ors. vs. State of U.P. and Ors. MANU/SC/0202/2004; State of Gujarat vs. Mirzapur Moti Kureshi Kassab Jamat and Ors. MANU/SC/1352/2005; Brihanmumbai Mahanagarpalika and Anr. vs. Willingdon Sports Club and Ors. MANU/SC/1190/2013; Siddhu Matriculation Hr. Secondary School vs. K. Shyam Sunder and Ors. MANU/SC/0915/2011; A.P. Dairy Development Corporation Federation vs. B. Narasimha Reddy and Ors. MANU/SC/1020/2011

NumberofPagesintheOriginalJudgment: 59

Case Note:

Constitution - Right to freedom of trade and business - Article 19 of Constitution of India and Food Safety and Standards Act, 2006 - Petitioner challenged Government action in respect of shutting down of abattoirs and slaughter houses throughout State - Whether Petitioners entitled for relief on ground that action of government affected their right to freedom of trade and business- Held, it appeared from record that State Government was regulating business and vending for ensuring lawful methods to be adopted and unlawful methods being prevented for carrying of trade and business of foodstuffs having animal origin - There was no dispute that food supply should conform to basics of hygiene and cleanliness and food safety - There was also no dispute that trade and business of foodstuffs having animal origin could be regulated including that through licensing provisions. - There was also no dispute of fact that trade and business of foodstuffs having animal origin had been permitted by appropriate regulations under relevant laws even prior to enforcement of2006 Act and Rules and Regulations framed there under - Thus in absence of any plea on behalf of State to impose prohibition of trade and business of foodstuffs having animal origin which also was not directly reflected in impugned Government Orders, there could not be any assumption or presumption of such prohibition or else that would violate constitutional rights and fundamental rights guaranteed under Constitution - Matter adjourned for further consideration with directions to state government. [47] and[80]

Facts:

1. This bunch of writ petitions raises a challenge to State Action in respect of shutting down of abattoirs and slaughter houses throughout the State, which in the opinion of the State Government were running unlawfully without complying with the provisions of the Prevention of Cruelty to Animals Act, 1960 read with the Prevention of Cruelty to Animals (Slaughter House) Rules, 2001, the provisions of the Food Safety and Standards Act, 2006 and the Rules, Regulations and orders relating thereto, the directions issued by the Hon'ble Apex Court in the case of Laxmi Narain Modi v. Union of India and Ors. - Writ Petition (C) No. 309 of 2003 and the orders passed finally in Writ Petition (C) No. 330 of 2001 (Common Cause v. Union of India & Ors.) on 17.02.2017 and the directions issued by the National Green Tribunal (N.G.T.).

1. The State Government under the exercise of its executive powers issued a Government Order on 22nd of March, 2017 containing directions to all administrative and police authorities as well as the local bodies concerned, as a consequence whereof several slaughter houses throughout the State which according to the State were running unlawfully and were either unregistered or unlicensed were shut down and sealed. The same resulted in directly affecting those who were

involved in the trade and profession of slaughtering as well as selling meat. The present bunch of writ petitions have arisen on account of the contingency aforesaid where various reliefs have been claimed; primarily to renew such licenses that were existing prior to the issuance of the Government Order by the respective local bodies and local self-government in the State, and for a further mandamus restraining the respondents not to interfere or create any hindrance in their trade and profession of either slaughtering or selling meat. Most of the writ petitions are by meat shop owners who are either engaged in the selling of buffalo meat or such bovines and others are venders of goat meat and poultry. Since, the writ petitions relating to the said relief are in majority, we would like to further mention that Writ Petition No. 8293(M/B) of 2017 - Mohd. Mustafa & 2 Ors. v. State of U.P. & Ors., has another prayer; praying for a mandamus to the Union of India and the Food Safety and Standards Authority to amend the IVth Schedule of the Food Safety and Standards Licensing and Registration of Food Business Regulations, 2011 with a further relief to construct requisite number of slaughter houses for facilitating the production and sale of meat and chicken throughout the State in rural and urban areas. The said writ petition impleads some of the Local Bodies in the State, the District Administration, the Union of India and the other authorities of the State.

Held, while allowing the appeal:

1. We therefore hereby direct the State Government to undertake this exercise through the said State Level Committee and make it known to the public at large through effective notifications and publications for everyone involved in such food trade or business to undertake such measures that may be required for either registration or licensing and at the same time, and ensure that such activities particularly where there are no facilities available, are not brought to a grinding halt, thereby interfering not only with the right of trade and business but also resulting in an impediment in supply of animal food stuff either in the urban or rural areas. This is necessary to prevent any chaotic situation but at the same time the State Government can take appropriate steps in accordance with law for preventing any unlawful activity. These plans could have been ensured had the State Government itself undertaken this exercise of looking to it's past performance and it's obligations to be discharged in future. To this extent, we find that the cause and apprehension expressed by the petitioners of

resulting in violation of rights therefore deserves to be noticed by the State Government itself. [76]

2. Accordingly, the State Level Committee so constituted by the State Government under the Office Memorandum dated 11.9.2012 is directed to thoroughly examine and assess all possibilities in this regard that have been indicated up till now and assist the State Government to undertake a policy decision in order to implement the directions of the Apex Court and the National Green Tribunal and the provisions of the Act and Rules in accordance with law as observed here-in-above. [77]

3. A copy of this judgment shall be circulated amongst all Divisional Commissioners and District Magistrates throughout the State as well as Local Bodies through it's respective Chairpersons to provide all such material and information to the State Government for the implementation of such a policy in accordance with law and the State Government will then take a decision in this regard including that of making budgetary allocations and finances that may be necessary for implementation of the directions referred to here-in-above. It is expected that the State Government and all it's authorities shall make an endeavour to study the social, the economic and the legal impact and the practicality of implementation with a view to implement the laws as a Model Social Welfare State under our Secular Constitution with the objective of ameliorating the conditions in this field of trade and business, hygiene, sanitation and healthy food for it's citizens on the anvil that it has the duty to do so. Any avoidance would ultimately result in denying livelihood to many as well as obstruction in animal food consumption that have now become a necessary part of life. This has to be kept in mind that the economic development of the State is being promoted by the Central Government as reflected in the documents on record coupled with the laws prevalent that do not prohibit rather permit the fostering of such activities that include poultries, fisheries, hatcheries, piggeries and the like which are essential and have a direct nexus with the consumption by the public at large. 79. The aforesaid exercise shall be undertaken by the State Level Committee and shall be reported to this Court by way of filing an affidavit by the next date fixed. 80. The matter shall come up for further consideration on 17.7.2017 which gives ample time to the State Government to gear up it's machinery for taking positive action in the matter in accordance with law. 8 1 . It shall be open to all the petitioners and such other persons to apply for registration or licenses as the case may be before the respective authorities under the 2006 Act and the 2011

Regulations and it shall be obligatory on the part of such authorities to assess and pass orders informing the applicants about the same. The Local Bodies shall be obliged to consider and grant No Objection Certificates as and where required under the 2011 Regulations. 82. In the event of any doubt about the exercise of such powers the matter shall be reported to the State Government forthwith without any delay and the Government shall be under an immediate obligation to convey it's directions for exercise of powers to the concerned authorities. Any slackness or any over doing shall be avoided while implementing these directions. 83. The learned Advocate General and the learned Counsel for the State are also requested to render their valuable opinion on the issue to the State Government that shall also be taken care of by the State Level Committee in coming to any conclusion. The petitioners through their representative organization can also espouse their cause before the State Government. [78]

Brihanmumbai Mahanagarpalika and Ors. vs. Willingdon Sports Club and Ors. (18.11.2013 - SC) : MANU/SC/1190/2013

Relative Section:

Food Safety And Standards Act, 2006 - Section 3(1)(n), Food Safety And Standards Act, 2006 - Section 3(ff)

Hon'bleJudges/Coram:

G.S. Singhvi and V. Gopala Gowda, JJ

Equivalent Citation: 2014(1) ABR438, AIR2014SC505, 2014(1) ALLMR400, 2014(1) BomCR571, 2014GLH (1)161, JT2013 (14)SC547, 2013(14)SCALE112, (2013)16SCC260, 2014 (1) SCJ 535, [2013] 14SCR848

Case Reference:

Sohrab Vakil (Lt. Col.) and Anr. v. B.G. Pimple and Anr., Writ Petition No. 4765 of 1984; W.I.A.A. Club Ltd and Anr. v. 1. Municipal Corporation of Gr. Bombay and Ors.; Union League Club v. Jhonson, 115 P.2d 425, 426, 18 Cal. 2d 275; State ex rel. City Loan and Savings Co. of Wapakoneta v. Zcllner, 13 N.E.2d 235, 238, 133 Ohio St. 263; Arthur Average Association for British Foreign and Colonia Ships, ex p Hargrove and Co. (1875) LR 10 Ch App 545 in at 546, 547; Narayan Gopal Karadkar v. Hanumant Ramrao Palkar MANU/MH/0111/1969:(1969)Maharashtra Law Journal 728;State

of Bombay v. Hospital Mazdoor MANU/SC /0200/1960:(1960)62Bom. L.R.
558; Balkrishna Karkera v. K.J. Mishra and Anr. MANU/MH/0041/1979:
AIR 1979 (Bombay) 198

NumberofPagesintheOriginalJudgment: 16

Case Note:

Food and Adulteration - License - Catering services - Section 394(1)(e)
of Bombay Municipal Corporation Act, 1888 - Present appeal filed against
order whereby High court relieved Respondents of obligation to take
licence under Section 394(1)(e) of Act - Whether Respondent was obliged
to take licence under Section 394(1)(e) for catering services provided by
it to members and their guests - Held, catering department of club which
prepares and serves/supplies food to members of club was covered by
definition of expression 'eating house' - Primary activity of club was to
provide sporting facilities to members, but supply of food was integral
part of such activity and catering department of club satisfies essential
component of facilities provided by club - One could take judicial notice of
fact that many members who avail sporting facilities remain on premises
for very long period - Therefore, articles of food become integral part of
their activities - Licensing system goes long way in ensuring food safety
thereby guaranteeing supply of fresh and safe food and preventing spread
of food borne diseases - Therefore, High Court was not right in relieving
Respondents of obligation to take licence under Section 394(1)(e) of Act -
Impugned order was set aside - Appeal allowed. [paras 13, 18, 27 and 28]

Facts:

1. The question which arises for consideration in this appeal filed against
order dated 29.9.2009 passed by the Division Bench of the Bombay High
Court in Writ Petition No. 2199/1999 is whether Respondent No. 1 is
obliged to take licence Under Section 394(1)(e) read with Part IV of
Schedule 'M' of the Bombay Municipal Corporation Act, 1888 (now titled as
'the Mumbai Municipal Corporation Act, 1888' - for short, 'the Act') for the
catering services provided by it to the members and their guests.

2. Respondent No. 1 provides various sporting facilities, viz., golf, tennis,
squash, billiards, badminton, etc., to its members. The Catering Department
of Respondent No. 1 provides catering services to the members and
occasionally to their guests. By order dated 21.11.1990, Appellant No. 2
called upon Respondent No. 1 to make an application for grant of licence
Under Section 394 of the Act for the eating house. The latter submitted
the application on 24.11.1990. Thereafter, Senior Sanitary Inspector of

Appellant No. 1 sent communication dated 3.12.1990 to Respondent No. 2 requiring him to submit various documents including NOCs from Assistant Engineer (Buildings and Facilities) and Executive Engineer (Buildings Proposals). In compliance of that letter, Respondent No. 2 furnished some of the documents. However, nothing appears to have been done for the next two years.

Held, while allowing the appeal:

1. In Balkrishna Karkera v. K.J. Mishra and Anr. MANU/MH/0041/1979 : AIR 1979 (Bombay) 198, learned Single Judge interpreted Section 394(1)(e)(i) read with Section 471 of the Act and observed:[25]

Now it is pertinent to note that although the expression "eating house" has been defined under the Bombay Municipal Corporation Act, the expression "catering establishment" has not been defined. It is true that the staff canteen run by Accused No. 2 was not open to the members of the public at large and the admission was restricted solely to the employees of the said Company. To that extent Mr. Shrikrishna would be justified in his submission that the staff canteen could not be termed as an "eating house." However, what is significant is the fact that Accused No. 2 has not been charged with carrying on an "eating house" but he has been charged for carrying on a catering establishment. "Catering establishment" is an expression which is wider in its connotation than the expression "eating house" and whether a staff canteen was open to the public or restricted only to a section of the public, it would still fall within the definition of a "catering establishment.

2. In our view, the aforesaid judgments of the Bombay High Court lay down correct law and ratio thereof deserves to be applied for interpreting Section 394 (1) (e) read with Part IV of Schedule 'M' of the Act. [26]

3. As a sequel to the above discussion, we hold that the Bombay High Court was not right in relieving the Respondents of the obligation to take licence Under Section 394(1)(e) of the Act. [27]

4. In the result, the appeal is allowed, the impugned order is set aside and the writ petition filed by the Respondents is dismissed with cost of Rs. 50,000. The amount of cost shall be deposited by Respondent No. 1 with Maharashtra State Legal Services Authority within a period of four weeks from today. [28]

5. Within four weeks from today, the Respondent shall file an application for grant of licence Under Section 394(1)(e) of the Act and produce the necessary documents. The application shall be processed and decided by

the competent Authority within next four weeks. [29]

6. It is made clear that Appellant No. 1 shall be free to initiate proceedings for imposition of penalty on Respondent No. 1 for its failure to take licence and pass appropriate order in accordance with law.

CHAPTER FOUR

Indian Dental Association U.P. State and Ors. vs. State of U.P. and Ors. (17.09.2012 – ALLHC) : MANU/UP/1686/2012

Relative Section:

Constitution Of India -Article 21,Article 47;

Food Safety And Standards Act, 2006 -Section 26,Section 26(1), Section 26(2)(v), Section 29(2), Section 30(1), Section 36, Section 36(2)(b), Section 37(1), Section 38(1)(b),Section 86,Section 89, Section 92

Hon'bleJudges/Coram:

Hon'ble Amar Saran, J. and Anurag Kumar, J.

Equivalent Citation: 2012(9)ADJ563, 2013(121)AIC301, 2012 (95) ALR 43, 2013 4 AWC3585All, 2013(4)Crimes51(All.)

Case Reference: nil

NumberofPagesintheOriginalJudgment:4

Case Note:

Food Safety and Standards Act, 2006 - Prohibition on sale of "gutka" and "pan masala" containing tobacco in light of provisions of Food Safety Act-- Regulation 2.3.4 of 2011 Regulations--Court would like to have response of State Government on next date of listing--As to steps taken within 14 days allowed by court--For ensuring compliance with directions of Central Government, Food Safety Act and Rules and Regulations framed there under--Restraining manufacture, sale and distribution of 'gutka' or other products containing tobacco as ingredient in State of U.P.--Failing this Court may have to consider need to issue mandamus to food business operators and State Government.

Facts:

A plea raised by the intervening food business operators in their intervention applications was that there was a special statute on the same subject viz. the "Cigarettes and other Tobacco products (Prohibition of Advertisement and Regulation of Trade and Commerce, Production, Supply and Distribution) Act 2003" on the same subject which would prevail over the Food Safety Act. As Regulation 2.3.4 issued by the Central government on 5.8.2011 was a later statute dealing with a specific issue, the prohibition on addition of tobacco and nicotine to a food product, whereas the Cigarettes and other Tobacco products Act 2003 only sought to restrain advertisements and to lay down other conditions to restrict the deleterious effects of tobacco consumption on youths etc. and other conditions relating to its trade and commerce, the Regulation which was later in point of time which dealt with a different subject, viz. the addition of tobacco or nicotine to food products should normally prevail over an earlier statute. Section 89 also enjoins that the provisions of the Food Safety Act would have overriding effect over other laws for the time being in force on the subject.

Held, while allowing the appeal:

In the light of the aforesaid discussion we would like to have the response of the State Government on the next listing as to the steps that have been taken in the 14 day period allowed by this Court for ensuring compliance of the directions of the Central government, the Food Safety Act and the regulations and rules framed there under for restraining the manufacture, sale and distribution of 'gutka' or other products containing tobacco as an ingredient in the State of U.P., failing which this Court may have to consider the need to issue a mandamus to the food business operators and the State government and its concerned authorities to follow the legal provisions imposing a ban on such products and to ensure compliance of Regulation 2.3.4 and the directions of the Central government in this regard. List this case on 10.10.2012. On that date compliance reports and necessary affidavits may also be submitted.

Suresh Kumar Gupta vs. Adjudication Authority/A.D.M., Basti and Ors. (31.08.2021 - ALLHC) : MANU/UP/2352/2021

Relative Section:

Food Safety And Standards Act, 2006 - Section 68(2), Section 76

Hon'bleJudges/Coram:

Dr. Kaushal Jayendra Thaker and Subhash Chand, JJ.

Equivalent Citation: 2022(232)AIC845, 2022 (118) ACC 512, 2021 (148) ALR 472, 2021 5 AWC5058 All , (2021)ILR 9All446, 2021 153 RD367

Case Reference: nil

NumberofPagesintheOriginalJudgment: 3

Case Note:

Food Safety and Standards Act, 2006 - Section 68(2)--Submission of appellant that no notice was served upon him and order under challenge was passed ex parte--Designated officer has not put his recommendations before the Commissioner of Food Safety for sanctioning prosecution against the appellant--Same officer was holding post of adjudicating officer which is violative of mandatory provisions of the Act--Signature of the; appellant on the order sheet has been disputed--Appellate I authority directed to decide the appeal afresh--Appeal disposed of accordingly. [5] to [10]

Facts:

The order of the authority below cannot be sustained for scrutiny before this Hon'ble Court as the same is passed without affording any reasonable opportunity to the appellant though of course notice was issued way back in the year 2017 but as per the appellant it was never served on the appellant. However, while entertaining this appeal we feel that the authority concerned has not mentioned the fact that the notice was received but in fact the appellant has not received the notice and could not put to his defence. The appellant is not a manufacturer and according to the appellant this aspect of the matter has not been looked into.

1. While condoning the delay we have directed the appellant to deposit 50% amount of fine. In compliance of the order dated 17.8.2021 the appellant has deposited 50% of the amount of fine i.e., ` 20,000/- on 27.8.2021. Receipt of deposit has been brought of on record as Annexure-SA-1 to the supplementary affidavit.(5)

2. The ground to set aside the order impugned is on hyper technical grounds as the principles of natural justice has not been followed by the quasi judicial authority while passing the said order. The appeal is allowed and the order impugned dated 22.6.2019 is set aside.

3. The allowing of this appeal is on technical ground that neither Sri S.K. Gupta nor his client was issued any notice. There is disputed question of fact that he was issued notice or yet to be issued. There is also dispute

regarding signature of the appellant in the order-sheet.

Held, while allowing the appeal:

We direct the parties to appear before the Adjudication Authority for adjudication of the case within one week from today as the respondent has raised dispute regarding his presence before the Adjudication Authority, Basti. Further he was never served with any notice.

1. Secondly, we have tried to balance the respondent by deposit of 50% of the amount under the order; impugned. The amount deposited is sought to be substantiated by the Supplementary affidavit. Normally we could not accept the affidavit in Court rather direct to file the same in the registry because the matter is being disposed of finally, hence we accept it and the same be taken on record. (9)

2. The deposit shall be subject to result of the appeal. The appellate authority will decide the matter afresh after providing full opportunity to the parties within a period of twelve weeks from today.(10)

3. We are thankful to the Counsel for the parties who have assisted the Court in disposing of this appeal finally.(11)

4. Let the record of Court below be sent back to the concerned Adjudication Authority, Basti.(12)

CHAPTER FIVE

Suresh Kumar Gupta vs. Adjudication Authority/ A.D.M., Basti and Ors. (31.08.2021 - ALLHC) : MANU/UP/2352/2021

Relative Section:

Food Safety And Standards Act, 2006 - Section 68(2), Section 76

Hon'bleJudges/Coram:

Dr. Kaushal Jayendra Thaker and Subhash Chand, JJ.

Equivalent Citation: 2022(232)AIC845, 2022 (118) ACC 512, 2021 (148) ALR 472, 2021 5 AWC5058 All , (2021)ILR 9All446, 2021 153 RD367

Case Reference: nil

NumberofPagesintheOriginalJudgment: 3

Case Note:

Food Safety and Standards Act, 2006 - Section 68(2)--Submission of appellant that no notice was served upon him and order under challenge was passed ex parte--Designated officer has not put his recommendations before the Commissioner of Food Safety for sanctioning prosecution against the appellant--Same officer was holding post of adjudicating officer which is violative of mandatory provisions of the Act--Signature of the; appellant on the order sheet has been disputed--Appellate I authority directed to decide the appeal afresh--Appeal disposed of accordingly. [5] to [10]

   Facts:

The order of the authority below cannot be sustained for scrutiny before this Hon'ble Court as the same is passed without affording any reasonable opportunity to the appellant though of course notice was issued way back in the year 2017 but as per the appellant it was never served on the appellant. However, while entertaining this appeal we feel that the authority concerned has not mentioned the fact that the notice was received but in fact the appellant has not received the notice and could not put to his defence. The appellant is not a manufacturer and according to the appellant this aspect of the matter has not been looked into.

1. While condoning the delay we have directed the appellant to deposit 50% amount of fine. In compliance of the order dated 17.8.2021 the appellant has deposited 50% of the amount of fine i.e., ` 20,000/- on 27.8.2021. Receipt of deposit has been brought of on record as Annexure-SA-1 to the supplementary affidavit.(5)

2. The ground to set aside the order impugned is on hyper technical grounds as the principles of natural justice has not been followed by the quasi judicial authority while passing the said order. The appeal is allowed and the order impugned dated 22.6.2019 is set aside.

3. The allowing of this appeal is on technical ground that neither Sri S.K. Gupta nor his client was issued any notice. There is disputed question of fact that he was issued notice or yet to be issued. There is also dispute regarding signature of the appellant in the order-sheet.

Held, while allowing the appeal:

We direct the parties to appear before the Adjudication Authority for adjudication of the case within one week from today as the respondent has raised dispute regarding his presence before the Adjudication Authority, Basti. Further he was never served with any notice.

1. Secondly, we have tried to balance the respondent by deposit of 50% of the amount under the order; impugned. The amount deposited is sought to be substantiated by the Supplementary affidavit. Normally we could not accept the affidavit in Court rather direct to file the same in the registry because the matter is being disposed of finally, hence we accept it and the same be taken on record. (9)

2. The deposit shall be subject to result of the appeal. The appellate authority will decide the matter afresh after providing full opportunity to the parties within a period of twelve weeks from today.(10)

3. We are thankful to the Counsel for the parties who have assisted the Court in disposing of this appeal finally.(11)

4. Let the record of Court below be sent back to the concerned Adjudication Authority, Basti.(12)

CHAPTER SIX

Tata Chemicals Ltd. vs. State of U.P. and Ors. (03.10.2017 - ALLHC) : MANU/UP/4028/2017

Relative Section:

Constitution Of India - Article 226; Food Safety And Standards Act, 2006 - Section 26, Food Safety And Standards Act, 2006 - Section 3(zf), Food Safety And Standards Act, 2006 - Section 46(4), Food Safety And Standards Act, 2006 - Section 52, Food Safety And Standards Act, 2006 - Section 70

Hon'bleJudges/Coram:

Dilip Gupta and Jayant Banerji, JJ.

Equivalent Citation: 2018(1)ADJ870, 2018 (128) ALR 497

Case Reference: Parakh Foods Ltd. vs. State of A.P. and Anr. MANU/SC/1228/2008

NumberofPagesintheOriginalJudgment: 8

Case Note:

Food adulteration - Misbranded - Packaging and Labelling - Sections 26 and 52 of Food Safety and Standards Act, 2006 (FSSA) - Present petition is filed seeking to quash order passed by Adjudicating Officer imposing penalty on petitioner under Sections 26 and 52 of FSSA for the reason that food product in question was misbranded and had violated regulation of Food Safety and Standards (Packaging and Labelling) Regulations , 2011 - Whether impugned order under challenge needs interference - Held, any information or pictorial device written, printed, or graphic matter may be displayed in label - It must not be in conflict with requirements of packaging regulations - Label shall not contain any statement, claim, design, device, fancy name or abbreviation which is false or misleading - Impugned order does not contain any finding that label contains any false or misleading statement - Offending portion does not contain any statement with regard to food that has been packaged - Unless product printed on label is related to food contained in the packet, there can be no misbranding - Impugned order is set aside - Petition allowed. [21]

Facts:

This petition seeks the quashing of the order dated 31 July 2013 passed by the Adjudicating Officer/Additional District Magistrate (F & R), Jaunpur (the Adjudicating Officer) by which a penalty of Rs. 1,25,000/- has been imposed on the petitioner-TATA Chemicals Limited (the petitioner) under Section 26/52 of the Food Safety and Standards Act, 2006 (the Act) for the reason that the food product in question was misbranded and had violated Regulation 2.3.1(5) of the Food Safety and Standards (Packaging and Labelling) Regulations, 2011 (the Packaging Regulations). It is stated that the proceedings were initiated against the petitioner after a seizure of a packet of TATA SALT' which also bore the words "HAVE YOU TRIED? TATA I-SHAKTI PULSES" and ultimately though the salt was found to be in conformity with the standards laid down in the Food Safety and Standards (Food Products Standards and Food Additives) Regulations, 2011 (the Additives Regulations), but the statementcontained in the packet referred to above was found to have violated the Packaging Regulations.

Held, while allowing the appeal:

23. Thus, unless the product printed on the label is related to the food contained in the packet, there can be no misbranding. It is also clear that the provisions of Section 3(zf) of the Act relating to 'misbranded food' would have no application in the present case as the article or food contained in the packet has not been offered or promoted for sale with false, misleading or deceptive claims. There has, therefore, been no violation of provisions of Regulation 2.3.1(5) of the Packaging Regulations.[23]

24. It is, therefore, not possible to sustain the impugned order dated 31 July 2013 passed by the Adjudicating Officer imposing penalty. It is, accordingly, set aside. The writ petition is, accordingly, allowed.[24]

CHAPTER SEVEN

Shyam Narain Pandey vs. State of U.P. and Ors. (18.02.2011 – ALLHC) : MANU/UP/0373/2011

Relative Section:

Food Safety And Standards Act, 2006 - Section 1, Food Safety And Standards Act, 2006 - Section 1(3), Food Safety And Standards Act, 2006 - Section 97, Food Safety And Standards Act, 2006 - Section 97(1); General Clauses Act 1897 - Section 6; Prevention Of Food Adulteration Act,1954 - Section 10, Prevention Of Food Adulteration Act,1954 - Section 10(4-A), Prevention Of Food Adulteration Act,1954 - Section 11(1)(c), Prevention Of Food Adulteration Act,1954 - Section 13(1), Prevention Of Food Adulteration Act,1954 - Section 23, Prevention Of Food Adulteration Act,1954 - Section 24, Prevention Of Food Adulteration Act,1954 - Section 3, Prevention Of Food Adulteration Act,1954 - Section 9

Hon'bleJudges/Coram: Pradeep Kant and Ritu Raj Awasthi, JJ.

Equivalent Citation: 2011(4) Crimes392, 2011(4)Crimes392(All.)

Case Reference: In re: Pepsico India Holdings (Pvt) Limited and Anr. v. State of U.P. and Ors. Writ Petitions No. 8254, 8255 and 8256 of 2010 (M/B)

NumberofPagesintheOriginalJudgment: 8

Case Note:

Food Adulteration - Licensing - Rule 4(1-A) and (1-B) of Uttar Pradesh Prevention of Food Adulteration Rules, 1976 -Section 3 Prevention of Food Adulteration Act, 1954 - Writ Petition challenged state government notification which provided for appointment of administrative officers as local health authorities of State, replacing technical persons having knowledge of medical and health matters namely Chief Medical Officer, Deputy Chief Medical Officers, Health Officers -Held - So far as appointment of officers of district officers as licensing authorities and local health authorities was concerned, Respondent state could not satisfy nor could show any provision under Act or the Rules which permitted such an appointment by State Government, that too by issuance of a Government Order, without amending Rules made under the PFA Act - Officers of district administration, who were supposed to have no knowledge of public health and ingredients used in various types of food products, process under which such food items were cooked or prepared and effect of such materials, namely, oils and chemicals used, on human body, couldn't be entrusted with this work - Such persons couldn't check adulteration as they neither could find out degree of adulteration nor could work out impact thereof on human and living beings - Chief Medical Officers and Additional Chief Medical Officers, who were experts in medical field, they being degree-holders in medical sciences, couldn't be replaced even in public interest with those who were non-experts in field - Besides that rules had not been amended, as was admitted by Respondent State and no Government Order or Office Order could be issued contrary to statutory rules - Since rules themselves prescribed and designated Chief Medical Officer/Additional Chief Medical Officer as licensing authority, this statutory prescription couldn't be withdrawn by executive order or by issuing a Government order - Thereby , appointment of City Magistrates or in their absence Deputy Collectors, nominated by District Magistrates under the PFA Act, 1954 as local health authorities for districts, couldn't be sustained, as authority had to be in consonance with provisions of Rules 2, 4 and 8 of the Rules of 1976 - On question whether notification issued under Section 1, Sub-section (3) of Act, 2006 meant a notification under Section 97, Sub-section (1) of said Act and had effect of repealing PFA Act and Rules or aforesaid notification was only a notification regarding commencement of said provision of Act, i.e date of its enforceability, which couldn't be treated to be a notification under Section 97(1) of the Act, 2006 issued by Central Government - Thereby , Government impugned orders were to remain in abeyance till final disposal of writ petition - State Government was directed to forthwith issue necessary orders/instructions restoring local health authorities as well as licensing authorities as per statutory provisions of PFA Act and Rules, 1976 - Orders/instructions so issued were to be subject to further orders of Court -Accordingly disposed off

Facts:

1. The issues raised in Writ Petition No. 4252 (M/B) of 2010 required the Court to consider whether the State Government could have issued the Government Orders dated 5.4.2010, 19.1.2010 and 7.5.2010, which, in substance provided for appointment of administrative officers as local health authorities of the State, replacing the technical persons having knowledge of medical and health matters, namely, Chief Medical Officer, Deputy Chief Medical Officers, Health Officers, etc. The said Government Orders are under challenge in these petitions.[4]

2. The decision to carve out a new Food and Drugs Administrative Department to shift the powers and responsibility from the persons having technical knowledge in the subject concerned i.e. Class I Medical Officers having knowledge of the impact of different chemicals and edible and non-edible items on human body, to the administrative machinery of district under the control of District Magistrate, having no knowledge about the technical and medical aspects of different items on the health of human-beings, has been assailed in the present writ petitions filed in the nature of public interest litigation.[5]

3. It is also the case of the Petitioner that in the absence of any competent and effective machinery being in existence, the business of edible items by the restaurants, hotels and factories, which are running without licence after 30th March, 2010, is a great danger to the life and health of the public in general.[6]

Held, while allowing the appeal:

After considering the arguments from both the sides, we are of the view that the question whether notification issued on 29.7.2010 under Section 1, Sub-section (3) of the Act, 2006 means a notification under Section 97, Sub-section (1) of the said Act and has the effect of repealing the PFA Act and the Rules or the aforesaid notification is only a notification regarding commencement of the said provision of the Act, i.e. the date of its enforceability, which cannot be treated to be a notification under Section 97(1) of the Act, 2006 issued by the Central Government, need be considered by a larger Bench, there being a conflict of opinion, as we, with deep regard, are not able to subscribe to the view expressed by the Division Bench in the case of Pepsico (supra) on this issue.

35. The issue whether the Food and Drugs Department can be separated or not, has not been addressed by us, as reference is being made to a larger Bench.[35]

36. We, therefore, for the reasons given above, direct that the Government Orders dated 5.4.2010, 19.1.2010 and 7.5.2010 shall remain in abeyance till the final disposal of these writ petition. The State Government is directed to forthwith issue necessary orders/instructions restoring the local health authorities as well as licensing authorities as per the statutory provisions of PFA Act and Rules, 1976. The orders/instructions so issued shall be subject to further orders of the Court.[36]

37. Further, on the plea of repeal of PFA Act and the Rules, 1976, we refer the following question for determination by a larger Bench:[37]

Whether the notification issued on 29.7.2010 under Section 1, Sub-section (3) of the Act, 2006 has the effect of repealing the Prevention of Food Adulteration Act, 1954 and the U.P. Prevention of Food Adulteration Rules, 1976 or the aforesaid notification is only a notification regarding commencement of the said provision of the Act i.e. the date of its enforceability, which cannot be treated to be a notification under Section 97(1) of the Act, 2006 issued by the Central Government?

38. Let the papers be placed before the Hon'ble Chief Justice for passing appropriate orders for referring the matter to the larger Bench.[38]

CHAPTER EIGHT

Toni and Ors. vs. State of U.P. and Ors. (28.09.2015 - ALLHC) : MANU/UP/1491/ 2015

Relative Section:

Code of Criminal Procedure, 1973 (CrPC) - Section 173; Section 190(1)(d); Section 378; Excise Act, 1910 - Section 12, Section 13, Section 15, Section 16, Section 4, Section 6, Section 60Section 61, Section 63, Section 72; Food Safety And Standards Act, 2006 - Section 21,Section 22, Section 3,Section 3(j), Section 31, Section 4, Section 40, Section 41, Section 42, Section 89, Section 92, Section 97; General Clauses Act 1897 - Section 6; Indian Penal Code 1860, (IPC) - Section 272; Section 273; Section 378; Section 379; Mines And Minerals (development And Regulation) Act, 1957 - Section 21, Section 4

Hon'bleJudges/Coram:

Vimlesh Kumar Shukla and Arvind Kumar Mishra-I, JJ.

Equivalent Citation: 2017(3)ADJ285, 2016 (97) ACC 880

Case Reference: Nil

NumberofPagesintheOriginalJudgment: 17

Case Note:

Criminal - First Information Report - Quashing thereof - Sections 60 and 72 of Excise Act, 1944 and Sections 272 and 273 of Indian Penal Code, 1860 - Present petition filed seeking quashing of First Information Report registered under Sections 60, 72 of Act and Sections 272, 273 of Code - Whether First Information Report was quashable - Held, liquor in question illegally smuggled was being adulterated with intention to sell such article - Therefore, Sections60, 72 of Act and Section 272, 273 of Code was attracted, to present case - First Information Report was not quashable - Petition dismissed. [16]

Facts:

Brief background of the case is that Sub-Inspector of U.P. Police- Raj Kumar Singh lodged First Information Report on 11.09.2013 at 6:30 hours mentioning therein that while the members of law enforcing agency were on routine petrol duty, on a tip off given by the informant that the petitioners have brought illicit liquor from Haryana in Chhota Hathi Vehicle and were engaged in adulterating the same with some intoxicant in the jungle situated at Village Chimau behind Shiv Mandir. At the said point of time, Excise Inspector and his associates also came and confirmed the information and both the teams raided the said place and found that the accused persons were engaged in illegal activities. On the spot one Tata Super S. No. HR 58A 5423 with 69 boxes with 628 bottles of country liquor in the name of Santra NVDistille Ries Ltd. Ambala Haryana was confiscated. Besides this one motorcycle and one plastic bag and other things were recovered. Based on the said raid that has been so conducted, present FIR in question has been lodged and same has impelled the petitioners to be before this Court.[2]

Held, while allowing the appeal:

17. The Judgment in the case of M/s. Pepsico India Holdings (Pvt.) Ltd. & Another v. State of U.P. and others 2010 (6) ALJ 30 is not at all applicable or attracted in the facts of the present case as in the said case, finding has been returned that there has been no allegation in the FIR that the petitioner-company or its employees or agents had kept its products with the intention to sell the same or knowing that the products are likely to be sold as food or drink or that the said products were exposed or offered for sale with the intention to sell the same on knowing that the products are likely to be sold as food or drink or the said products are for exports or for sale.

18. Once such is the background of the case, then the principles laid down therein is not at all applicable or attracted in the case in hand. In view of this, writ petition sans merit and is accordingly, dismissed.

Jvl Agro Industries Ltd. vs. Union of India and Ors. (13.10.2015 - ALLHC) : MANU/UP/1604/2015

Relative Section:

Constitution Of India - Article 19(1)(g), Article 226;

Food Safety And Standards Act, 2006 - Section 10, Section 10(5), Section 3(1)(e), Section 3(1)(q), Section 30, Section 31Section 32, Section 32(3), Section 32(4), Section 32(4)(c), Section 42(3), Section 47, Section 59, Section 9, Section 92(2)(o)

Hon'bleJudges/Coram:

Amreshwar Pratap Sahi and Attau Rahman Masoodi, JJ.

Equivalent Citation: 2015(11)ADJ1, 2015(156)AIC915, 2015 (113) ALR 669, 2016 1 AWC834All

Case Reference: nil

NumberofPagesintheOriginalJudgment: 16

Case Note:

Food Adulteration - Suspension of licence - Jurisdiction of Court - Section 10(5) of Food Safety and Standards Act, 2006 - Present petition filed against order whereby Licensing Authority suspended license for manufacturing product in question by Petitioner on ground that sample which was collected by Respondents was found to be sub-standard and unsafe and had tested positive for rancidity - Whether appeal lies before Commissioner or not - Held, no challenge raised to extent of powers to be exercised by Chief Executive Officer as Commissioner of Food Safety under sub-section (5) of Section 10 of Act - Appeal would be maintainable before Chief Executive Officer under sub-section (5) of Section 10 of Act - Appeal filed before Commissioner was not forum available to Petitioner and Petitioner ought to have approached Authority in terms of Section 10(5) of Act - Petition disposed off. [31] and[32]

Facts:

The petitioner has challenged the impugned suspension order dated 2nd July, 2015, as contained in Annexure No. 1 to this writ petition. An objection has been taken by the opposite parties, namely by the Standing Counsel as well as Assistant Solicitor General of India that against the said suspension order an appeal lies under Section 32(4)(C) of the Food Safety and Standards Act, 2006. Sri Gupta has submitted that he has already preferred an appeal but an objection has been taken by the opposite parties vide their reply on behalf of Food Safety and Standards Authority of India Act that appeal is not maintainable in the case of the petitioner. For the reasons enumerated in the reply there appears contradictory standard between statutory provision as well as the grounds taken by the Central Licensing Authority viz-a-viz Food Safety and Standards Authority of India.

Held, while allowing the appeal:

1. We are, therefore, of the opinion that the appeal filed before the State Food Safety Commissioner was not the forum available to the petitioner and the petitioner ought to have approached the authority as referred to hereinabove in terms of Section 10(5) of the Act.[32]

2.Having said so and having found that the appeal before the State Food Safety Commissioner to be not maintainable against the order of the Central Licensing Authority dated 2.7.2015 the proceedings before him, therefore, are without authority and without jurisdiction. Consequently, we provide that it shall be open to the petitioners to file an appropriate appeal before the authority concerned as noted above within a period of ten days from the date of availability of the certified copy of this order. In the event the petitioners also apply for an interim relief the same shall be considered and orders passed in accordance with law within a week thereafter.[33]

3. However, in view of the fact and the findings that we have arrived at hereinabove and the urgency of the matter we also provide that as directed under the impugned order further prosecution of the petitioners shall not be undertaken unless the said application is finally disposed of by the Appellate Authority as directed hereinabove.[34]

4. The relief of challenge to the interim order dated 16.7.2015 is rendered infructuous in view of what has been concluded above.[35]

5. With the aforesaid directions the writ petition stands disposed of.

CHAPTER TEN

Deen Mohammad vs. State of U.P. and Ors. (10.09.2018 - ALLHC) : MANU/UP/4844/ 2018

Relative Section:

Constitution Of India - Article 14, Article 19, Article 21, Article 246, Article 246 (1), Constitution Of India - Article 254, Article 254 (2), Article 254(1);

Food Safety And Standards Act, 2006 - Section 1 (2), Section 100, Section 19 to 36(1) ,Section 48 to, Section 89, Section 92 to Section 98,

General Clauses Act 1897 - Section 6;

Uttar Pradesh Kshettra Panchayats And Zila Panchayats Adhiniyam, 1961 - Section 197, Section 239

Hon'bleJudges/Coram:

Shashi Kant Gupta and Ajit Kumar, JJ.

Equivalent Citation: 2018(11)ADJ682, 2019(2) ALJ 131, 2018 (131) ALR 312, 2018 6 AWC6248All

Case Reference:

The Security Association of India vs. Union of India (UOI) MANU/ SC/0596/2014; Welfare Assocn. A.R.P., Maharashtra and Anr. vs. Ranjit P. Gohil and Ors. MANU/SC/0129/2003; Zaverbhai Amaidas vs. The State of Bombay MANU/SC/0040/1954; Salem Advocate Bar Association, Tamil Nadu vs. Union of India (UOI) MANU/SC/0450/2005; Rameshwari Devi and Ors. vs. Nirmala Devi and Ors. MANU/SC/0714/2011

NumberofPagesintheOriginalJudgment:14

Case Note:

Food Safety and Standards Act, 2006 - Sections 89 and 97 (2), (3)--Food Safety and Standards (Licensing and Registration of Food Business) Regulations, 2011--Regulations 1.2.1 (5), (6) and 2.1.1 (4)--U.P. Kshettra Panchayats and Zila Panchayats Adhiniyam, 1961--Sections 239 (2) and 197--Licence-Grant of for food business--Petitioner running his meat shop in the village after obtaining licence from State Licensing Authority under the Act of 2006--Respondent No. 3 passed order directing the petitioner to close his meat shop as he had not obtained licence from Zila Panchayat--Petitioner had also applied for licence to Zila Panchayat and was granted no objection certificate from Village Development Officer and Station House Officer--Petitioner retail dealer and petty food business operator--No registering authority notified for granting registration to Petty Food Business Operator--Petitioner charged ` 2,000 towards licence fee as against ` 100 prescribed--Power exercised by the 3rd respondent in passing impugned order dated 3.10.2017--Clear transgression of authority and cannot be approved--Wrong done unlawfully requires to be remedied--Petitioner entitled to exemplary cost of ` 2,00,000 to be paid by 3rd respondent within six weeks--Petitioner free to carry on his business as per terms and conditions of the licence--Writ petition allowed. [29] to [33], [44], [45], [51] and [52]

Facts:

The brief facts of the case as narrated in the writ petition are that the petitioner is resident of Village-Jasoi, Police Station-Titavi, District-Muzaffarnagar and running his meat shop in the aforesaid village. To carry out of the aforesaid business, the petitioner had applied for issuing license before the respondent No. 3-Additional Chief Officer, Zila Panchayat, Muzaffarnagar and pursuance to the aforesaid application, respondent No. 3 has called detailed report from the concerned Gram Panchayat as well as police station of the area. On 5.9.2017, S.H.O. of Police station Titavi, District-Muzaffarnagar has submitted 'No Objection Certificate' before the respondent No. 3 with a recommendation to grant of license to the petitioner. The Secretary/Village Development Officer, Vikas Kshetra Jasoi, Block Baghara, District Muzaffarnagar has also given 'No Objection Certificate' in respect of the shop of the petitioner. 'No Objection Certificate' given by both the authorities have been annexed as Annexure-3 to the writ petition. It has been further submitted that the petitioner has applied for license for running the meat shop under The Food, Safety and

Standards Act, 2006 (in short 'FSS Act, 2006'). Thereupon, the respondent No. 4 issued license No. 12717065000300 in the name of M/s. Din Meat Shop on 28.9.2017 and thereafter the petitioner started to run his shop peacefully. It has been further stated in the writ petition that a false complaint was made before the respondent No. 2 by one Vikram Saini alleging that the petitioner is running meat shop illegally in the concerned area without any authority and license. Pursuant to the aforesaid false complaint, the respondent No. 2 has called for report from the respondent No. 4 and in pursuance thereof, the respondent No. 4 submitted report on 25.10.2017 stating that after getting 'No Objection Certificate' from the Secretary, Village Development Officer and concerned Station House Office, the license No. 12717065000300 dated 28.9.2017 was issued to the petitioner which was valid for a period of one year. Thereafter the respondent No. 3 has passed the impugned order dated 3.10.2017 stating that since the petitioner has not obtained license from the Zila Panchayat, the petitioner was directed to close the meat shop. Hence, the present writ petition has been filed by the petitioner.

Held, while allowing the appeal:

51. In the present case, the food business operator, namely, the petitioner, we are constrained to hold, was wholly illegally, deprived of his livelihood for almost whole of the year, the period for which license was to operate, but for illegal and wholly misplaced assumption of authority by the 3rd respondent. The period of the license is just coming to expire by 27th September, 2018 and thus the petitioner was made to suffer huge financial loss and business prospects for none of his fault An unnecessary litigation has been forced upon him. Under the circumstances, we are of the view that the petitioner is entitled to exemplary cost of Rs. 2,00,000/- to be paid by the 3rd respondent to the petitioner within a period of six weeks from the date of production of a certified copy of this order, failing which, the same shall be recovered as arrears of land revenue.[51]

52. The petitioner is free to carry on his business as per the terms and conditions of the license and apply for registration/renewal of license in future as law may permit under the FSS Act, 2006 and the Regulations, 2011 framed there under.[52]

53. Before we part with the case, we feel it appropriate to request that in case if the registering authority has not been notified by the State Government as is required under Regulations, 2011 read with Section 31 (2) of the FSS Act, 2006, the State Government shall take all endeavour to

designate and notify the Registering Authority forthwith as required under the Act (supra).[53]

54. In the result, the writ petition succeeds and is allowed as above.

CHAPTER ELEVEN

NKGSB Cooperative Bank Limited vs. Subir Chakravarty and Ors. (25.02.2022 - SC) : MANU/SC/0247/2022

Relative Section:

Andhra Pradesh Reorganisation Act, 2014 - Section 86;Arms Act 1959 - Section 24A, Section 24B, Section 43; Army Act, 1950 - Section 47; Banning Of Unregulated Deposit Schemes Act, 2019 - Section 31; Bihar Reorganisation Act, 2000 - Section 80; Central Goods And Services Tax Act, 2017 - Section 107, Section 108,Section 112, Section 5; Section 2(g); Chemical Weapons Convention Act, 2000 - Section 22, Section 23, Section 24, Section 37; Child And Adolescent Labour (prohibition And Regulation) Act, 1986 - Section 17A; Children Act, 1960 - Section 56; Code of Civil Procedure, 1908 (CPC) - Order XXVI Rule 17, Code of Criminal Procedure, 1973 (CrPC) - Section 12; Section 154; Section 165; Section 17; Section 284; Section 34; Section 55; Conservation Of Foreign Exchange And Prevention Of Smuggling Activities Act, 1974 - Section 12; Constitution Of India - Article 154, Article 226, Article 227, Article 311, Article 311(1), Article 53; Customs Act, 1962 - Section 129D, Section 129DA, Section 28J, Section 5; Delhi Police Act, 1978 - Section 12,Section 122, Section 147, Section 20, Section 21, Section 25, Section 3, Section 58, Section 64, Section 70; Delhi Rent Act, 1995 - Section 44; Employee's Compensation Act, 1923 - Section 2(1), Section 2(f); Export (quality Control And Inspection) Act, 1963 - Section 10K, Section 10M, Section 13; Food Safety And Standards Act, 2006 - Section 30; Foreign Trade (development And Regulation) Act, 1992 -

Section 11, Section 15, Section 16,Section 6; Fugitive Economic Offenders Act, 2018 - Section 8; General Clauses Act 1897 - Section 3(5);

Guardians And Wards Act, 1890 - Section 4A; Hotel-receipts Tax Act, 1980 - Section 23; Human Immunodeficiency Virus And Acquired Immune Deficiency Syndrome (prevention And Control) Act, 2017 - Section 45; Indian Coconut Committee Act, 1944 - Section 2(a); Indian Evidence Act, 1872 - Section 121; Indian Penal Code 1860, (IPC) - Section 165; Indian Penal Code 1860, (IPC) - Section 376; Indian Succession Act, 1925 - Section 195; Industrial Disputes Act, 1947 - Section 39; Industrial Employment (standing Orders) Act, 1946 - Section 14A; Industrial Relations Code, 2020 - Section 100; Insurance Act, 1938 - Section 110A, Insurance Act, 1938 - Section 110B, Insurance Act, 1938 - Section 34H; Legal Metrology Act, 2009 - Section 54; Mahatma Gandhi National Rural Employment Guarantee Act, 2005 - Section 26; Maintenance And Welfare Of Parents And Senior Citizens Act 2007 - Section 22; Manipur Land Revenue And Land Reforms Act, 1960 - Section 166, Manipur Land Revenue And Land Reforms Act, 1960 - Section 5, Manipur Land Revenue And Land Reforms Act, 1960 - Section 68, Manipur Land Revenue And Land Reforms Act, 1960 - Section 7, Manipur Land Revenue And Land Reforms Act, 1960 - Section 84, Manipur Land Revenue And Land Reforms Act, 1960 - Section 93, Manipur Land Revenue And Land Reforms Act, 1960 - Section 95, Manipur Land Revenue And Land Reforms Act, 1960 - Section 96; Narcotic Drugs And Psychotropic Substances Act, 1985 - Section 41; National Security Act, 1980 - Section 14; New Delhi Municipal Council Act, 1994 - Section 328, New Delhi Municipal Council Act, 1994 - Section 46; Orphanages And Other Charitable Homes (supervision And Control) Act, 1960 - Section 5; Passports Act, 1967 - Section 21; Police Act, 1861 - Section 2, Police Act, 1861 - Section 7; Prevention Of Illicit Traffic In Narcotic Drugs And Psychotropic Substances Act, 1988 - Section 13; Prevention Of Money-laundering Act, 2002 - Section 17; Prisons Act, 1894 - Section 22, Prisons Act, 1894 - Section 48, Prisons Act, 1894 - Section 8; Punjab Reorganisation Act, 1966 - Section 79; Railways Act, 1989 - Section 93; Requisitioning And Acquisition Of Immovable Property Act, 1952 - Section 17, Requisitioning And Acquisition Of Immovable Property Act, 1952 - Section 23; Right To Fair Compensation And Transparency In Land Acquisition, Rehabilitation And Resettlement Act, 2013 - Section 43; Securitisation And Reconstruction Of Financial Assets And Enforcement Of Security Interest Act, 2002 - Section 13, Securitisation And Reconstruction Of Financial

Assets And Enforcement Of Security Interest Act, 2002 - Section 13(2), Securitisation And Reconstruction Of Financial Assets And Enforcement Of Security Interest Act, 2002 - Section 13(4), Securitisation And Reconstruction Of Financial Assets And Enforcement Of Security Interest Act, 2002 - Section 14, Securitisation And Reconstruction Of Financial Assets And Enforcement Of Security Interest Act, 2002 - Section 14(1), Securitisation And Reconstruction Of Financial Assets And Enforcement Of Security Interest Act, 2002 - Section 14(1-A), Securitisation And Reconstruction Of Financial Assets And Enforcement Of Security Interest Act, 2002 - Section 14(1A), Securitisation And Reconstruction Of Financial Assets And Enforcement Of Security Interest Act, 2002 - Section 14(2), Securitisation And Reconstruction Of Financial Assets And Enforcement Of Security Interest Act, 2002 - Section 14(3), Securitisation And Reconstruction Of Financial Assets And Enforcement Of Security Interest Act, 2002 - Section 38, Securitisation And Reconstruction Of Financial Assets And Enforcement Of Security Interest Act, 2002 - Section 6(b); Security Interest (enforcement) Rules, 2002 - Rule 2(a), Security Interest (enforcement) Rules, 2002 - Rule 8, Security Interest (enforcement) Rules, 2002 - Rule 8(3), Security Interest (enforcement) Rules, 2002 - Rule 9; Suppression Of Immoral Traffic In Women And Girls Act, 1956 - Section 14; Unlawful Activities (prevention) Act, 1967 - Section 42, Unlawful Activities (prevention) Act, 1967 - Section 43A; Uttar Pradesh Consolidation Of Holdings Act, 1953 - Section 48; Uttar Pradesh Reorganisation Act, 2000 - Section 81; Wild Life (protection) Act, 1972 - Section 5

Hon'bleJudges/Coram:

A.M. Khanwilkar and C.T. Ravikumar, JJ.

Equivalent Citation:2022(3)ABR182, 2022(233)AIC220, AIR2022SC1325, 2022(2)ALLMR854,I(2022) BC612(SC), 2022(2)BomCR410, 2022 (1) CCC 381 , 2022GLH(2)1, 2022/INSC/238, 2022 (2) RCR (Civil) 414, (2022)10SCC286, 2022 (2) SCJ 319, [2022]171SCL310(SC), [2022]1SCR1177

Case Reference:

Muhammed Ashraf and Ors. v. Union of India (UOI) MANU/KE/0456/2008; Federal Bank Limited v. A.V. Punnus MANU/KE/1086/2013; Sakiri Vasu v. State of U.P. and Ors. MANU/SC/8179/2007; Dattatreya Moreshwar Pangarkar v. The State of Bombay and Ors. MANU/SC/0014/1952; Sangram Singh v. Election Tribunal, Kotah and Ors. MANU/SC/0044/1955;

A.S.T. Arunachalam Pillai v. Southern Roadways (Private) Ltd. MANU/SC/0249/1960; S. Krishnaswamy Mudaliar and Ors. v. P.S. Palani Pillai and Ors. MANU/TN/0237/1957; B. Veeraswamy and Ors. v. State of Andhra Pradesh represented by its Secretary, Public Works and Transport Department, Hyderabad and Ors. MANU/AP/0192/1959; R.G. Jacob v. Union of India (UOI) MANU/SC/0140/1962; Government of A.P. and Ors. v. N. Ramanaiah MANU/SC/0815/2009; Raghunath Sahai v. Sarup Singh MANU/UP/0147/1962; Ram Narain and Ors. v. Director of Consolidation and Ors. MANU/UP/0050/1965; Laxminarayan Sarangi v. State of Orissa and Ors. MANU/OR/0002/1963; Mahadev Prasad Roy v. S.N. Chatterjee and Ors. MANU/BH/0097/1954; Gurmukh Singh v. Union of India (UOI), New Delhi MANU/PH/0102/1963; Rao Shiv Bahadur Singh and Ors. v. The State of Vindhya Pradesh MANU/SC/0081/1953; Lalit Mohan Das v. Advocate-General, Orissa MANU/SC/0019/1956; O.P. Sharma and Ors. v. High Court of Punjab and Haryana MANU/SC/0571/2011; Satheedevi v. Prasanna and Ors. MANU/SC/0367/2010; Hiralal Rattanlal and Ors. v. State of U.P. and Ors. MANU/SC/0553/1972; Dipak Babaria and Ors. v. State of Gujarat and Ors. MANU/SC/0052/2014; V.S. Sunitha v. Federal Bank Ltd.; S. Chandramohan and Anr. v. The Chief Metropolitan Magistrate, Egmore, Chennai and Ors. MANU/TN/2503/2014 : 2014-5-L.W. 620; Rahul Chaudhary v. Andhra Bank and Ors.; J. Marks Exim (India) Pvt. Ltd. v. Punjab National Bank; Mahadev Govind Gharge and Ors. v. Special Land Acquisition Officer, Upper Krishna Project, Jamkhandi, Karnataka MANU/SC/0597/2011 : (2011) 6 SCC 321; Federal Deposit Ins. Corporation v. Winton, C.C.A. Tenn. MANU/FEST/0054/1942 : 131 F.2d 780; Slegel v. Slegel 135 N.J. Eq. 5 : 37 A.2d 57; Doherty v. King, Tex. Civ. App. 183 S.W.2d 1004; Donohue v. Zoning Bd. of Appeals of Town of Norwalk 155 Conn. 550 : 235 A.2d 643; Authorised Officer, Indian Bank v. D. Visalakshi and Anr. MANU/SC/1303/2019 : (2019) 20 SCC 47

NumberofPagesintheOriginalJudgment:25

Case Note:

Banking - Possession of Secured Assets and documents - Appointment of Advocate for such purpose - Section 14(1A) of the Securitisation and Reconstruction of Financial Assets and Enforcement of Security Interest Act, 2002 - Whether District Magistrate or the Chief Metropolitan Magistrate can appoint an advocate and authorise him/her to take possession as provided for in the statute?

Facts:

The Bombay High Court vide its relevant judgment opined that the advocate, not being a subordinate officer to the CMM or DM, such appointment would be illegal. Against this decision, four separate appeals were filed by the concerned parties. On the other hand, the High Court of Madras took a contrary view that the advocate is regarded as an officer of the court and, thus, subordinate to the CMM or the DM. Against this decision, a special leave petition was filed by the borrowers. The High Courts of Kerala and Delhi have taken the same view. Hence the present appeals to adjudicate on whether Advocate can be appointment as one authorised to take possession of secured assets and connected document.

Held, while disposing the Appeals:

It is well established that an advocate is a guardian of constitutional morality and justice equally with the Judge. He has an important duty as that of a Judge. He bears responsibility towards the society and is expected to act with utmost sincerity and commitment to the cause of justice. He has a duty to the court first. As an officer of the court, he owes allegiance to a higher cause and cannot indulge in consciously misstating the facts or for that matter conceal any material fact within his knowledge.[39]

There is no reason to assume that the advocate so appointed by the CMM/DM would misuse the task entrusted to him/her and that will not be carried out strictly as per law or it would be a case of abuse of power. Rather, going by the institutional faith or trust reposed on advocates being officers of the court, there must be a presumption that if an advocate is appointed as commissioner for execution of the orders passed by the CMM/DM under Section 14(1) of the 2002 Act, that responsibility and duty will be discharged honestly and in accordance with Rules of law.[42]

A fortiori, the judgment and order of the Bombay High Court impugned in the present appealsis declared as not a good law. Whereas, the conclusion of the three High Courts, namely, High Courts of Kerala, Madras and Delhi on the question under consideration upheld.[45]

The appeals filed by the secured creditors are allowed. Resultantly, the impugned judgment and order passed by the Bombay High Court is set aside and the subject writ petition stands dismissed.The special leave petition filed by the borrowers against the impugned judgment and order of the Madras High Court is delinked for being heard for admission, on the limited issue regarding compliance or non-compliance of Clauses (i) to (ix) of Section 14 of the 2002 Act in the fact situation of the present case.[47]

CHAPTER TWELVE

The State of Arunachal Pradesh and Ors. vs. Ramchandra Rabidas and Ors. (04.10.2019 - SC) : MANU/ SC/1383/2019

Relative Section:

Code of Criminal Procedure, 1973 (CrPC); Food Safety And Standards Act, 2006 - Section 26, Food Safety And Standards Act, 2006 - Section 30, Food Safety And Standards Act, 2006 - Section 55; General Clauses Act 1897 - Section 26; Indian Income-tax Act, 1922 - Section 52; Indian Penal Code, 1860 (IPC) - Section 5, Indian Penal Code, 1860 (IPC) - Section 177, Indian Penal Code, 1860 (IPC) - Section 188, Indian Penal Code, 1860 (IPC) - Section 272, Indian Penal Code, 1860 (IPC) - Section 273, Indian Penal Code, 1860 (IPC) - Section 279, Indian Penal Code, 1860 (IPC) - Section 297, Indian Penal Code, 1860 (IPC) - Section 300, Indian Penal Code, 1860 (IPC) - Section 304, Indian Penal Code, 1860 (IPC) - Section 304A, Indian Penal Code, 1860 (IPC) - Section 328, Indian Penal Code, 1860 (IPC) - Section 336, Indian Penal Code, 1860 (IPC) - Section 337, Indian Penal Code, 1860 (IPC) - Section 338; Mines and Minerals (Development and Regulation) Act, 1957; Motor Vehicles (Amendment) Act, 1994 - Section 40; Motor Vehicles Act, 1988 - Section 112, Motor Vehicles Act, 1988 - Section 112(2), Motor Vehicles Act, 1988 - Section 132(1), Motor Vehicles Act, 1988 - Section 133, Motor Vehicles Act, 1988 - Section 134, Motor

Vehicles Act, 1988 - Section 183, Motor Vehicles Act, 1988 - Section 183(1), Motor Vehicles Act, 1988 - Section 184, Motor Vehicles Act, 1988 - Section 185, Motor Vehicles Act, 1988 - Section 186, Motor Vehicles Act, 1988 - Section 187, Motor Vehicles Act, 1988 - Section 188, Motor Vehicles Act, 1988 - Section 208, Motor Vehicles Act, 1988 - Section 208(1), Motor Vehicles Act, 1988 - Section 208(2), Motor Vehicles Act, 1988 - Section 208(3), Motor Vehicles Act, 1988 - Section 209; Probation Of Offenders Act, 1958 - Section 4

Hon'bleJudges/Coram:

Indu Malhotra and Sanjiv Khanna, JJ.

Equivalent Citation: IV(2019)ACC229(SC), 2019ACJ3063, 2020(207)AIC248, 2020(205)AIC243, AIR 2019 SC4954, 2019(6)ALD307, 2020 (1) ALD(Crl.) 125 (SC), 2020 (110) ACC 303, 2020 (139) ALR 761, 2020 (1) ALT (Crl.) 401 (A.P.), 2020(3)BLJ196, 2020CriLJ122, 2019/INSC/1126, 2019(4)J.L.J.R.244, 2019(4) JKJ420[SC], 2019(4)JLJ290, 2019(4)KLJ373, 2019(4)KLT646, 2020(2)MLJ(Crl)100, 2020(II)MPJR(SC)13, 2019 (3) N.C.C.792, 2019(4)PLJR162, 2020(1)RCR(Civil)41, 2019(13)SCALE669, (2019)10SCC75, [2019]15SCR771, 2019(4)TAC707, 2021(1)UC447

Case Reference:

M.K. Kunhimohammed v. P.A. Ahmedkutty and Ors. MANU/SC/0477/1987; T.S. Baliah v. T.S. Rengachari MANU/SC/0238/1968; Dalbir Singh v. State of Haryana MANU/SC/0345/2000; Rattan Singh v. State of Punjab MANU/SC/0226/1979; State of Karnataka v. Krishna alias Raju MANU/SC/0483/1987; Guru Basavaraj @ Benne Settappa v. State of Karnataka MANU/SC/0682/2012; The New India Assurance Co. Ltd. v. C. Padma and Anr. MANU/SC/0704/2003; Deepal Girishbhai Soni and Ors. v. United India Insurance Co. Ltd., Baroda MANU/SC/0246/2004; Vimla Devi and Ors. v. National Insurance Company Limited and Ors. MANU/SC/1290/2018; Naresh Giri v. State of M.P. MANU/SC/4297/2007; Rathnashalvan v. State of Karnataka MANU/SC/7024/2007; Alister Anthony Pareira v. State of Maharashtra MANU/SC/0015/2012; N.K.V. Bros. (P) Ltd. v. M. Karumai Ammal and Ors. MANU/SC/0321/1980; Gopal Singh v. State of Uttarakhand MANU/SC/0140/2013; State of Karnataka v. Sharanappa Basnagouda Aregoudar MANU/ SC / 0214 /2002; National Insurance Company Ltd. v. Annappa Irappa Nesaria and Ors. MANU/SC/7093/2008; Gottumukkala Appala Narasimha Raju and Ors. v. National Insurance Co. Ltd. and Anr. MANU/SC/0981/2007; State of Maharashtra v.Sayyed Hassan

Criminal Appeal No. 1195-1207 of 2018; State (NCT of Delhi) v. Sanjay

NumberofPagesintheOriginalJudgment: 15

Case Note:

Motor Vehicles - Road traffic offences - Prosecution thereto - High Court issued directions that road traffic offences shall be dealt with only under provisions of Motor Vehicles Act, 1988 (M.V. Act), and in holding that in cases of road traffic or motor vehicle offences, prosecution under provisions of Indian Penal Code, 1860 was without sanction of law, and recourse to provisions of Indian Penal Code would be unsustainable in law - Hence, present appeal - Whether in cases of road traffic or motor vehicle offences, prosecution would lie both under Indian Penal Code and MV Act.

Facts:

The High Court issued directions that road traffic offences shall be dealt with only under the provisions of the Motor Vehicles Act, 1988 (M.V. Act), and in holding that in cases of road traffic or motor vehicle offences, prosecution under the provisions of Indian Penal Code, 1860 was without sanction of law, and recourse to the provisions of the Indian Penal Code would be unsustainable in law.

Held, while allowing the appeal:

(i) There was no conflict between the provisions of the Indian Penal Code and the MV Act. Both the statutes operate in entirely different spheres. The offences provided under both the statutes were separate and distinct from each other. The penal consequences provided under both the statutes were also independent and distinct from each other. The ingredients of offences under the both statutes, were different, and an offender could be tried and punished independently under both statutes. The principle that the special law should prevail over the general law, has no application in cases of prosecution of offenders in road accidents under the Indian Penal Code and M.V. Act. [6]

(ii) The High Court had given a contradictory finding by holding on the one hand that the provisions of the Code of Criminal Procedure must succumb to the provisions of the M.V. Act, as executive authorities cannot take away a beneficial provision under a special law enacted by Parliament, while on the other hand, it had opined that the M.V. Act was not a complete code in itself, and there was no complete bar to investigate road traffic offences under the provisions of Code of Criminal Procedure. [14]

(iii) This Court had consistently held that the M.V. Act, 1988 is a complete code in itself in so far as motor vehicles were concerned.

However, there was no bar under the M.V. Act or otherwise, to try and prosecute offences under the Indian Penal Code for an offence relating to motor vehicle accidents. On this ground as well, the impugned judgment was liable to be set aside. [15]

(iv) Therefore, set aside the directions issued by the High Court to issue appropriate instructions to their subordinate officers to prosecute offenders in motor vehicle accidents only under the provisions of the Motor Vehicles Act, 1988 and not the Indian Penal Code. [17]

Ratio Decidendi: A prosecution, if otherwise maintainable, would lie both under the Indian Penal Code and the MV Act, since both the statutes operate with full vigour, in their own independent spheres.

Disposition: Appeal Allowed

Pepsico India Holdings (Pvt) Ltd. and Ors. vs. State of U.P. and Ors. (08.09.2010 – ALLHC) : MANU/UP/3189

Relative Section:

Code of Criminal Procedure, 1973 (CrPC) - Section 156(3); Section 167; Section 4; Constitution Of India - Article 14, Article 21;

Food Safety And Standards Act, 2006 - Section 1, Section 100, Section 19, Food Safety And Standards Act, 2006 - Section 20, Food Safety And Standards Act, 2006 - Section 21 to Section 29, Food Safety And Standards Act, 2006 - Section 29(1), Food Safety And Standards Act, 2006 - Section 3, Food Safety And Standards Act, 2006 - Section 3(zw), Food Safety And Standards Act, 2006 - Section 31 to Section 35, Food Safety And Standards Act, 2006 - Section 40 to Section 42, Food Safety And Standards Act, 2006 - Section 48, Food Safety And Standards Act, 2006 - Section 49, Food Safety And Standards Act, 2006 - Section 50 to Section 98, Food Safety And Standards Act, 2006 - Section 97(1), Food Safety And Standards Act, 2006 - Section 97(2);

General Clauses Act 1897 - Section 5(3), Section 6; Indian Penal Code 1860, (IPC) - Section 2; Section 272; Section 273; Section 419; Section 420,Section 467; Section 468,Section 471; Section 5; Maharashtra Control Of Organised Crime Act, 1999 - Section 23, Section 25; Prevention Of Food Adulteration Act,1954 - Section 10, Section 11, Section 16, Section 5, Section 7; Transplantation Of Human Organs And Tissues Act, 1994 - Section 13(3)(iv), Transplantation Of Human Organs And Tissues Act,

1994 - Section 22

Hon'bleJudges/Coram:

Rajiv Sharma and Syed Nazim Husain Zaidi, JJ.

Equivalent Citation: : 2011(2)Crimes250, 2011(2)Crimes250(All.)

Case Reference:

Jeewan Kumar Raut and Another v. Central Bureau of Investigation 2009 (7) UJ SC 3135; Jamruddin Ansari v. CBI MANU/SC/0924/2009 : (2009) 6 SCC 316; State of M.P. v. Kedia Leather and Liquor Ltd and Ors. MANU/SC/0625/2003 : (2003) 7 SCC 389; Basti Sugar Mills Co. Ltd. v. State of U.P. and Another (1979) 2 SCC 86; Charm v. Excise Inspector MANU/KE/0541/2005 : 2006 (1) KLT 511; North East Pure Drinks Pvt Ltd v. State of Assam; Jatinder Kumar Jain v. State of Punjab 2008 (2) FAC 437

NumberofPagesintheOriginalJudgment: 17

Case Note:

Prevention Of Food Adulteration – Criminal Offence and FIR to be registered vide State Govt, Order - it gives unfettered powers to the authorities to initiate action against violators or suspected violators for food adulteration and misbranding by invoking Sections 272/273 IPC by registering FIRs. prosecution would lie both under Indian Penal Code and Food Safety And Standards Act, 2006

Facts:

The facts of the case are that the petitioner Pepsico India Holdings Private Limited, is a company registered under the provisions of the Companies Act, 1956. The company is engaged in the business of manufacturing of soft drinks inter alia under the brand name of PEPSI, Lehar, 7UP, Slice and Miranda etc. The company is aggrieved by the issuance of the Government Order dated 11.5.2010 issued by the State Government as it gives unfettered powers to the authorities to initiate action against violators or suspected violators for food adulteration and misbranding by invoking Sections 272/273 IPC by registering FIRs. After the issuance of the aforesaid Government Order, various products of; the Company were seized from the godown and FIRs were registered against the officers/agents of the company under Sections 272/273 IPC and Section 7/16 of the Prevention of Food Adulteration Act, 1954 [hereinafter referred to as the 'PFA Act'].

Held, while allowing the appeal:

1. In view of the aforesaid crystal clear legal proposition and particular provisions under the FSSA we are in agreement with the arguments

advanced by the petitioner's Counsel that for adulteration of food or misbranding, after coming into force of the provisions of FSSA vide notification dated 29th July, 2010, the authorities can take action only under the FSSA as it postulates an over riding effects over all other food related law including the PFA Act. In view of the specific provisions under the FSSA, the offences relating to adulteration of food that are governed under the FSSA after July 29, 2010 are to be treated as per the procedures to be followed for drawing and analysis of samples as have been provided for. The provisions of penalties and prosecution have also been provided therein. Therefore, before launching any prosecution against an alleged offence of food adulteration, it is necessary for the concerned authorities to follow the mandatory requirements as provided under Sections 41 and 42 of the FSSA and, therefore, the police have no authority or jurisdiction to investigate the matter under FSSA. Section 42 empowers the Food Safety Officer for inspection of food business, drawing samples and sending them to Food Analyst for analysis. The Designated Officer, after scrutiny of the report of Food Analyst shall decide as to whether the contravention is punishable with imprisonment or fine only and in the case of contravention punishable with imprisonment, he shall send his recommendations to the Commissioner of Food Safety for sanctioning prosecution. Therefore, invoking Sections 272 and 273 of the Indian Penal Code in the matter relating to adulteration of food pursuant to the impugned Government order is wholly unjustified and non est. Furthermore, it appears that the impugned Government Order has been issued without application of proper mind and examining the matter minutely and thus the State Government travelled beyond the jurisdiction. [27]

2. In view of the aforesaid discussions, the writ petitions are allowed. The impugned G.O. dated 11.5.2010 issued by the State Government contained in Annexure-1 to the writ petition is hereby quashed. Consequently, the FIR dated 11.8.2010 registered as case crime No. 392 of 2010 under Sections 272/273 IPC, PS Cantt. District Varanasi, FIR dated 11.8.2010 in Case Crime No. 144 of 2010 registered at PS Rohaniya. District Varanasi and the FIR registered as case crime No. 244 of 2010, PS Khuldaoad, District Allahabad are also hereby quashed. The concerned Magistrates shall immediately pass necessary orders for forthwith release of all the petitioners, who are in jail.[28]

CHAPTER FOURTEEN

Gauri Maulekhi vs. State of Uttarakhand and Ors. (14.08.2018 - UCHC) : MANU/UC/0593/2018

Relative Section:

Food Safety And Standards Act, 2006 - Section 31, Food Safety And Standards Act, 2006 - Section 92(2)(o); Prevention Of Cruelty To Animals Act, 1960 - Section 1(1), Prevention Of Cruelty To Animals Act, 1960 - Section 11, Prevention Of Cruelty To Animals Act, 1960 - Section 35, Prevention Of Cruelty To Animals Act, 1960 - Section 38

Hon'bleJudges/Coram:

Rajiv Sharma and Manoj Kumar Tiwari, JJ

Equivalent Citation: 2019(9)FLT74

Case Reference: nil

NumberofPagesintheOriginalJudgment: 10

Case Note:

Environment - Necessary Directions - Public interest litigation filed by Petitioner for issuance of necessary directions to union of India for framing of rules - Whether court could issue necessary direction to union of India for framing of Rules - Held, Ordinarily court would not direct Union of India for framing of Rules but since, it appeared that recommendations have already been made by Law Commission in its 269th Meeting, court deem it fit to request Union of India to frame Prevention of Cruelty to Animals (Egg Laying Hens) Rules well as the Prevention of Cruelty to Animals (Broiler Chicken) Rules - Petition disposed of with directions. [20], [21]

Facts:

Case of the petitioner, in a nutshell, is that the State Government, though, has issued the communication on 18. 4.2013 (Annexure No. 5) but the same, till date, has not been enforced in letter and spirit. It is also the case of petitioner that Chapter VII of the Transport of Animal Rules,1978 has not been strictly enforced by the State Government .Petitioner has also drawn the attention of this Court to the recommendations made by the Law Commission of India in its 269th Report which is at page No.208 of the paper book. On the issue of Transportation and House-keeping of Egg-laying hens (layers) and Broiler Chickens, the Law Commission has stated as under:-

"Indian ethos has always considered animals quintessential aspect of human living. Kautilya's Arthshastra talks extensively of animal welfare. For example, it prohibited killing or injuring protected species and animals in reserved parks and sanctuaries. Village headman was responsible for preventing cruelty to animals and a person found treating an animal cruelly could be restrained in any manner."

Animals find mention in religion, folk tales and mythology, in direct and indirect ways. They define ways of existence and life events. It is believed that animals can communicate and have sentiments as well. It is also significant that humans always had a symbiotic relation with the animals.

Worldwide, the chickens have been commercially trait selected for two reasons, that of egg production (layers) and meat production (broilers). The Law Commission in this report has examined the issues pertaining to both, the layers and broilers. Specifically in layer birds, the issues relate to disposal of male chicks and housing of egg laying hens. In case of broilers, the issue of trait selection, housing, transport and slaughter of the birds, have been examined."

Held, while allowing the appeal:

Accordingly, the present petition is disposed of by issuing the following mandatory directions: -

A. The respondent-State is directed to strictly enforce the letter dated 18.4.2013 (Annexure No. 5) in letter and spirit forthwith. Usage of battery cage facilities is banned throughout the State of Uttarakhand. Sufficient space should be allowed for the housing of each egg laying hen to permit the bird to spread its wings, stand up straight, turn round without touching another bird or the side of the cage. The bird must have access to nest box.

B. The State Government is directed to ensure that while transporting the poultry, the containers are properly cleaned and sterilized before the poultry is placed in them.

C. The poultry shall not be exposed to the sunlight, rain and direct blast of air during transport.

D. There shall be a ban on transportation of poultry when the temperature exceeds 25 degree Celsius or when the temperature falls below 15 degree Celsius.

E. The day-old chicks and turkey poults shall be packed and dispatched as per Rule 78 of the Transport of Animal Rules, 1978. The chicks or poults shall be properly fed and watered before and during transportation.

F. The State Government is directed to ensure that the containers used to transport poultry shall be made of such material which shall not collapse or crumble and they shall be well ventilated and designed to protect the health of poultry by giving it adequate space and safety. The size of the container should be as prescribed under Rule 83(d) of the Rules of 1978.

G. The wire mesh or a net of any material shall not be used as a bottom for the containers.

H. No poultry shall be transported continuously for more than 6 hours and whole batch shall be inspected at every 6 hours interval. The transportation shall not remain stationary for more than 30 min and during this period, it shall be parked in shade and arrangements shall be made for feeding and watering.

I. All precautions against fire shall be taken and provision of fire extinguishers in transfer is also ordered to be provided.

J. The Union of India is requested to consider framing the Prevention of Cruelty to Animals (Egg Laying Hens) Rules well as the Prevention of Cruelty to Animals (Broiler Chicken) Rules, on the basis of the recommendations made by the Law Commission in its 269th Meeting within six months.

The Court places on record its appreciation for the assistance rendered to it by the petitioner who appeared in person.[22]

All pending applications stand disposed of accordingly.

CHAPTER FIFTEEN

Swami Achyutanand Tirth and Ors. vs. Union of India (UOI) and Ors. (05.08.2016 - SC) : MANU/SC/0857/2016

Relative Section:

Food Safety and Standards Act, 2006 - Section 3, Food Safety and Standards Act, 2006 - Section 7A, Food Safety and Standards Act, 2006 - Section 16, Food Safety and Standards Act, 2006 - Section 18(1), Food Safety and Standards Act, 2006 - Section 19, Food Safety and Standards Act, 2006 - Section 23, Food Safety and Standards Act, 2006 - Section 31, Food Safety and Standards Act, 2006 - Section 50, Food Safety and Standards Act, 2006 - Section 51, Food Safety and Standards Act, 2006 - Section 52, Food Safety and Standards Act, 2006 - Section 53, Food Safety and Standards Act, 2006 - Section 55, Food Safety and Standards Act, 2006 - Section 56, Food Safety and Standards Act, 2006 - Section 57, Food Safety and Standards Act, 2006 - Section 58, Food Safety and Standards Act, 2006 - Section 59, Food Safety and Standards Act, 2006 - Section 60, Food Safety and Standards Act, 2006 - Section 61, Food Safety and Standards Act, 2006 - Section 62, Food Safety and Standards Act, 2006 - Section 63, Food Safety and Standards Act, 2006 - Section 54, Food Safety and Standards Act, 2006 - Section 65, Food Safety and Standards Act, 2006 - Section 89, Food Safety and Standards Act, 2006 - Section 91, Food Safety and Standards Act, 2006 - Section 92(2), Food Safety and Standards Act, 2006 - Section 97(2); Indian Penal Code, 1860 (IPC) - Section 272, Indian Penal Code, 1860 (IPC) - Section 273; Food Safety and Standard Rules, 2011; Constitution of India - Article 21;

Food Safety and Standards (Licencing and Registration of Food Businesses) Regulations, 2011 - Regulation 2.1, Food Safety and Standards (Licencing and Registration of Food Businesses) Regulations, 2011 - Regulation 2.1.13; Food Safety and Standards (Packaging and Labeling) Regulations, 2011; Food Safety and Standards (Food Products, Standards and Food Additives) Regulations, 2011 - Regulation 1.2

Hon'bleJudges/Coram:

T.S. Thakur, C.J.I., R. Banumathi and U.U. Lalit, JJ.

Equivalent Citation: 2016(165)AIC234, AIR2016SC3626, 2016(4)AJR519, 2016 (96) ACC 429, 2016 5 AWC 4353SC, 2016(5)BomCR245, 2016(3)Crimes288(SC), 2016/INSC/575, 2016(3)J.L.J.R.446, 2016 (4) KHC 260, 2016(3)KLT780, 2016-5-LW585, 2016(II)OLR768, 2016(4)PLJR68, 2016(3)RCR(Criminal)994, 2016(7)SCALE583, (2016)9SCC699, 2016 (7) SCJ 473, [2016]4SCR849

Case Reference: nil

NumberofPagesintheOriginalJudgment: 11

Case Note:

LETTER PETITION AND PIL MATTER for Food Adulteration – Criminal matter - News of "National Survey on adulteration of Milk" was reported in various newspapers including 'The Hindu', 'Business Line', 'Times of India', 'Indian Express' and other newspapers, the clippings of which are filed in IA No. 2 of 2012, an application for impleadment filed by one Manisha Shah. The result of the above survey confirms that the samples of milk were diluted with water or found to have been adulterated with chemicals. Nutritional value of milk is compromised by mixing water and other harmful agents. Adulteration of milk with water is used to increase the volume of milk and brings down the nutritional value, and contaminated water in adulterated milk can cause gastroenteritis, stomach ailments, etc. Adulteration of milk with chemicals like caustic soda and detergents etc. is very serious. Prolonged consumption of milk adulterated with chemicals may affect vital body organs and may pose health risk to the infants, children and also adults.

Facts:

1. The present writ petition is filed in public interest by the Petitioners highlighting the menace of growing sales of adulterated and synthetic milk in different parts of the country. The Petitioners are residents of the State of Uttarakhand, Uttar Pradesh, Rajasthan, Haryana and NCT of Delhi and have accordingly shown concern towards the sale of adulterated milk in their

States. However, the issue of food safety being that of national importance, Union of India has also been made a party-Respondent. The Petitioners allege that the concerned State Governments and Union of India have failed to take effective measures for combating the adulteration of milk with hazardous substance like urea, detergent, refined oil, caustic soda, etc. which adversely affects the consumers' health and seek appropriate direction.

2. The Petitioners have relied on a report dated 02.01.2011 titled "Executive Summary on National Survey on Milk Adulteration, 2011" released by Foods Safety and Standards Authority of India (FSSAI) which concluded that on a national level, 68.4 per cent of milk being sold is adulterated and it is alleged that the worst performers in the survey were Bihar, Chhattisgarh, Odisha, West Bengal, Mizoram, Jharkhand and Daman and Diu, where adulteration in milk was found up to 100%. In the States of Uttarakhand and Uttar Pradesh 88% of milk samples were found adulterated. According to the Petitioners, milk is the only source of nourishment for infants and a major part of the diet for growing children in tender age and if no effective measure is taken to ensure the purity of milk, health of the children will be adversely affected. The Petitioners pleaded inaction and apathy on the part of the Respondents to take appropriate measure to Rule out sale and circulation of synthetic milk and milk products across the country which according to the Petitioners has resulted in violation of fundamental rights of the Petitioners and public at large guaranteed Under Article 21 of the Constitution of India. The Petitioners, therefore, seek for a writ of mandamus directing Union of India and the concerned State Governments to take immediate effective and serious steps to Rule out the sale and circulation of synthetic/adulterated milk and the milk products like ghee, mawa, cheese, etc.

Held, while allowing the appeal:

Considering the seriousness of the matter and in the light of various orders passed by this Court, the Writ Petition is disposed of with the following directions and observations:

i. Union of India and the State Governments shall take appropriate steps to implement Food Safety and Standards Act, 2006 in a more effective manner.

ii. States shall take appropriate steps to inform owners of dairy, dairy operators and retailers working in the State that if chemical adulterants like pesticides, caustic soda and other chemicals are found in the milk, then stringent action will be taken on the State Dairy Operators or retailers or all the persons involved in the same.

iii. State Food Safety Authority should also identify high risk areas (where there is greater presence of petty food manufacturer/business operator etc.) and times (near festivals etc.) when there is risk of ingesting adulterated milk or milk products due to environmental and other factors and greater number of food samples should be taken from those areas.

iv. State Food Safety Authorities should also ensure that there is adequate lab testing infrastructure and ensure that all labs have/obtain NABL accreditation to facilitate precise testing. State Government to ensure that State food testing laboratories/district food laboratories are well-equipped with the technical persons and testing facilities.

v. Special measures should be undertaken by the State Food Safety Authorities (SFSA) and District Authorities for sampling of milk and milk products, including spot testing through Mobile Food Testing Vans equipped with primary testing kits for conducting qualitative test of adulteration in food.

vi. Since the snap short survey conducted in 2011 revealed adulteration of milk by hazardous substances including chemicals, such snap short surveys to be conducted periodically both in the State as well as at the national level by FSSAI.

vii. For curbing milk adulteration, an appropriate State level Committee headed by the Chief Secretary or the Secretary of Dairy Department and District level Committee headed by the concerned District Collector shall be constituted as is done in the State of Maharashtra to take the review of the work done to curb the milk adulteration in the district and in the State by the authorities.

viii. To prevent adulteration of milk, the concerned State Department shall set up a website thereby specifying the functioning and responsibilities of food safety authorities and also creating awareness about complaint mechanisms. In the website, the contact details of the Joint Commissioners including the Food Safety Commissioners shall be made available for registering the complaints on the said website. All States should also have and maintain toll free telephonic and online complaint mechanism.

ix. In order to increase consumer awareness about ill effects of milk adulteration as stipulated in Section 18(1)(f) the States/Food Authority/ Commissioner of Food Safety shall inform the general public of the nature of risk to health and create awareness of Food Safety and Standards. They should also educate school children by conducting workshops and teaching them easy methods for detection of common adulterants in food, keeping in mind indigenous technological innovations (such as milk adulteration detection strips etc.)

x. Union of India/State Governments to evolve a complaint mechanism for checking corruption and other unethical practices of the Food Authorities and their officers.

CHAPTER SIXTEEN

The State of Maharashtra and Ors. vs. Sayyed Hassan Sayyed Subhan and Ors. (20.09.2018 - SC) : MANU/SC/1021/2018

Relative Section:

Food Safety and Standards Act, 2006 - Section 26, Food Safety and Standards Act, 2006 - Section 30, Food Safety and Standards Act, 2006 - Section 55, Food Safety and Standards Act, 2006 - Section 68; General Clauses Act 1897 - Section 26; Mines and Minerals (Development and Regulation) Act, 1957; Indian Penal Code, 1860 (IPC) - Section 188, Indian Penal Code, 1860 (IPC) - Section 272, Indian Penal Code, 1860 (IPC) - Section 273, Indian Penal Code, 1860 (IPC) - Section 328

Hon'bleJudges/Coram:

S.A. Bobde and L. Nageswara Rao, JJ.

Equivalent Citation: 2019(195)AIC129, AIR2018SC5348, 2019 (1) ALD(Crl.) 223 (SC), 2019 (106) ACC 1005, 2018ALLMR(Cri)5367, 2018 (3) ALT (Crl.) 365 (A.P.), IV(2018)CCR365(SC), 2018(4) Crimes167(SC), 2018/INSC/848, 2018(4)J.L.J.R.205, 2018 (4) KHC 647, 2018(4)PLJR297, 2018(4)RCR(Criminal)341, 2018(11)SCALE317, (2019)18SCC145, 2018(3)UC2227

Case Reference:

State (NCT of Delhi) v. Sanjay MANU/SC/0761/2014 : (2014) 9 SCC 772; T.S. Baliah v. T.S. Rengachari MANU/SC/0238/1968 : (1969) 3 SCR 65; State of Bihar v. Murad Ali Khan MANU/SC/0470/1988 : (1988) 4 SCC 655; State of Rajasthan v. Hat Singh MANU/SC/0006/2003 : (2003) 2 SCC 152

NumberofPagesintheOriginalJudgment:4

Case Note:

CRIMINAL MATTERS - MATTERS FOR/AGAINST QUASHING OF CRIMINAL PROCEEDINGS - Crimes were registered pursuant to complaints filed by the Food Safety Officers for violation of the said notification dated 18.07.2013 against the Respondents who were either transporting, stocking and/or selling the prohibited goods.

Facts:

1. First Information Reports (FIRs) were registered for transportation and sale of Gutka/Pan Masala for offences punishable Under Sections 26 and 30 of the Food and Safety Standards Act, 2006 (hereinafter referred to as the 'FSS Act') and Sections 188, 272, 273 and 328 of the Indian Penal Code, 1860 (hereinafter referred to as the 'IPC'). The Respondents in the above appeals filed Criminal Writ Petitions and Criminal Applications in the High Court of Bombay for quashing the FIRs. The High Court quashed the criminal proceedings against the Respondents and declared that the Food Safety Officers can proceed against the Respondents under the provisions of Chapter X of the FSS Act. Aggrieved thereby, the State of Maharashtra is before us.

2. The High Court framed two questions for consideration. They are:

i. Whether the Food Safety Officers can lodge complaints for offences punishable under the Indian Penal Code?

ii. Whether the acts complained amounted to any offence punishable under the provisions of the Indian Penal Code?

Held, while allowing the appeal:

Regarding the second point as to whether offences Under Section 188, 272, 273 and 328 have been made out against the Respondents, we have considered the submissions made by the learned Additional Solicitor General for the State of Maharashtra and the learned Senior Counsel appearing for the Respondents. Without going into details of the submissions made, we find that points that were not argued before the High Court were raised by both sides. We suggested to the parties that the matters have to be considered afresh by the High Court by permitting both sides to raise all contentions which were canvassed before us. There was no serious objection by both sides to the remand of the matters back to the High Court. The only request made by the learned Senior Counsel for the Respondents is that no coercive action should be taken against the Respondents during the pendency of Criminal Writ Petitions and the Criminal Applications before the High Court.

1. We remand the matters to the High Court to consider the Criminal Writ Petitions and Criminal Applications afresh in respect of the second point framed i.e. whether offences Under Section 188, 272, 273 and 328 of the Indian Penal Code are made out in the FIRs which are the subject matter of the cases. No coercive action be taken against the Respondents till the disposal of the Criminal Writ Petitions and the Criminal Applications by the High Court.[10]

2. With the aforesaid observations, the appeals are disposed of.

CHAPTER SEVENTEEN

Trilok Chand vs. State of Himachal Pradesh (01.10.2019 - SC) : MANU/SC/1832/2019

Relative Section:

Prevention of Food Adulteration Act, 1954 - Section 2(ix), Prevention of Food Adulteration Act, 1954 - Section 7, Prevention of Food Adulteration Act, 1954 - Section 16(1); Food Safety and Standards Act, 2006 - Section 51, Food Safety and Standards Act, 2006 - Section 52

Hon'bleJudges/Coram:

Navin Sinha and Sanjiv Khanna, JJ.

Equivalent Citation: 20221FAC678, 2019(II)OLR1072, (2020)10SCC763

Case Reference:

T. Barai v. Henry Ah Hoe and Anr. MANU/SC/0123/1982 : (1983) 1 SCC 177; Calder v. Bull

NumberofPagesintheOriginalJudgment:2

Case Note:

CRIMINAL MATTERS - CRIMINAL MATTERS IN WHICH SENTENCE AWARDED IS MORE THAN FIVE YEARS. Under Sections 51 and 52 of the Food Safety and Standards Act, 2006, the maximum penalty for sub-standard food or branding is only fine. The State has opposed the appeal submitting that there are concurrent findings of misbranding in accordance with the law, as it then stood on the date of occurrence

Facts:

1. The Appellant assails his conviction Under Section 16(1)(a)(i) read with Section 7 of the Prevention of Food Adulteration Act, 1954 (for short

"the Act") sentencing him to three months' imprisonment along with fine of Rs. 500/-.

2. The Food Inspector visited the shop of the Appellant and purchased three packets of rewari weighing 3 x 700 gms each on payment of Rs. 60/- for which receipt was granted. The necessary formalities were thereafter complied with by the Food Inspector. The sample along with Form VI was sent to the public analyst who opined that the product was misbranded within the meaning of Section 2(ix)(k) punishable under the Act.

3. The Appellant assailed his conviction unsuccessfully in appeal and his revision too has been dismissed by the High Court.

4. Learned Counsel for the Appellant made a very short submission before us relying on an order dated 10.03.2016 in Criminal Appeal No. 214 of 2006. He submits that Under Sections 51 and 52 of the Food Safety and Standards Act, 2006, the maximum penalty for sub-standard food or branding is only fine. He, therefore, submits that the conviction may be set aside on that ground.

5. Learned Counsel for the State has opposed the appeal submitting that there are concurrent findings of misbranding in accordance with the law, as it then stood on the date of occurrence.

Held, while allowing the appeal:

We have considered the respective submissions. In Criminal Appeal No. 214 of 2006, this Court relied on a decision in T. Barai v. Henry Ah Hoe and Anr. MANU/SC/0123/1982 : (1983) 1 SCC 177 wherein it was opined that since the amendment was beneficial to the Accused persons, it could be applied with respect to earlier cases as well which are pending in the Court observing:

22. It is only retroactive criminal legislation that is prohibited Under Article 20(1). The prohibition contained in Article 20(1) is that no person shall be convicted of any offence except for violation of a law in force at the time of the commission of the act charged as an offence prohibits nor shall he be subjected to a penalty greater than that which might have been inflicted under the law in force at the time of the commission of the offence. It is quite clear that insofar as the Central Amendment Act creates new offences or enhances punishment for a particular type of offence no person can be convicted by such ex post facto law nor can the enhanced punishment prescribed by the amendment be applicable. But insofar as the Central Amendment Act reduces the punishment for an offence punishable Under Section 16(1)(a) of the Act, there is no reason why the Accused

should not have the benefit of such reduced punishment. The Rule of beneficial construction requires that even ex post facto law of such a type should be applied to mitigate the rigour of the law. The principle is based both on sound reason and common sense. This finds support in the following passage from Craies on Statute Law, 7th Edn., at pp. 388-89:

A retrospective statute is different from an ex post facto statute. "Every ex post facto law." said Chase, J., in the American case of Calder v. Bull "must necessarily be retrospective, but every retrospective law is not an ex post facto law. Every law that takes away or impairs rights vested agreeably to existing laws is retrospective, and is generally unjust and may be oppressive; it is a good general Rule that a law should have no retrospect, but in cases in which the laws may justly and for the benefit of the community and also of individuals relate to a time antecedent to their commencement: as statutes of oblivion or of pardon. They are certainly retrospective, and literally both concerning and after the facts committed. But I do not consider any law ex post facto within the prohibition that mollifies the rigour of the criminal law, but only those that create or aggravate the crime or increase the punishment or change the Rules of evidence for the purpose of conviction.... There is a great and apparent difference between making an unlawful act lawful and the making an innocent action criminal and punishing it as a crime.

In view of the same, the present appeal is allowed in part and the sentence imposed upon the Appellant is modified by imposing a fine of Rs. 5,000/- only, which shall be deposited within 30 days before the Trial Court. On deposit of the amount, the bail bonds of the Appellant shall stand discharged. [7]

Trimurti Traders vs. State of U.P. (03.03.2014 - ALLHC) : MANU/UP/0653/2014

Relative Section:

Food Safety And Standards Act, 2006 - Section 3(1)(j), Food Safety And Standards Act, 2006 - Section 3(1)(n), Food Safety And Standards Act, 2006 - Section 3(1)(y), Food Safety And Standards Act, 2006 - Section 31(1)

Hon'bleJudges/Coram:

D.Y. Chandrachud, C.J. and Dilip Gupta, J.

Equivalent Citation: 2014(3) ALJ 187

Case Reference: nil

NumberofPagesintheOriginalJudgment: 2

Case Note:

The food business to be registered under the provisions of the Food Safety and Standards Act, 2006. The petitioners submitted their objections on 13 January 2014. By the impugned order dated 16 January 2014, the objections have been rejected and it has been held that all traders such as the petitioners situated within the precincts of the Mandi Samiti would have to obtain licences/registration by 4 February 2014.

Facts:

1. The petitioners are registered brokers in the Krishi Utpadan Mandi Samiti, Maudaha, Hamirpur. The petitioners claim to carry out the work of brokers or dalals. According to them, in the ordinary course of business, they arrange contracts for the purchase or sale of agricultural produce on behalf of their principals against the payment of commission or remuneration, whether in cash or kind as specified under Section 2(b) of the U.P. Krishi Utpadan Mandi Adhiniyam, 1964. On 10/13 December, 2013, the Additional District Magistrate (Finance and Revenue), Hamirpur, passed an order requiring persons in the food business to be registered under the provisions of the Food Safety and Standards Act, 2006. The petitioners submitted their objections on 13 January 2014. By the impugned order dated 16 January 2014, the objections have been rejected and it has been held that all traders such as the petitioners situated within the precincts of the Mandi Samiti would have to obtain licences/registration by 4 February 2014.

Held, while allowing the appeal:

The Food Safety and Standards Act, 2006 was enacted to consolidate the law relating to food and, inter alia, to regulate the manufacture, storage, distribution, sale and import and to ensure availability of safe and wholesome food for human consumption and for matters incidental thereto. Having regard to the underlying object, and principles, Parliament has broadly defined the expressions, 'food', 'food business' and 'ingredients'. In this view of the matter, the order of the District Magistrate requiring registration does not suffer from any error. The petition is, accordingly, dismissed.

CHAPTER EIGHTEEN

Trimurti Traders vs. State of U.P. (03.03.2014 – ALLHC) : MANU/UP/0653/2014

Relative Section:

Food Safety And Standards Act, 2006 - Section 3(1)(j), Food Safety And Standards Act, 2006 - Section 3(1)(n), Food Safety And Standards Act, 2006 - Section 3(1)(y), Food Safety And Standards Act, 2006 - Section 31(1)

Hon'bleJudges/Coram:

D.Y. Chandrachud, C.J. and Dilip Gupta, J.

Equivalent Citation: 2014(3) ALJ 187

Case Reference: nil

NumberofPagesintheOriginalJudgment: 2

Case Note:

The food business to be registered under the provisions of the Food Safety and Standards Act, 2006. The petitioners submitted their objections on 13 January 2014. By the impugned order dated 16 January 2014, the objections have been rejected and it has been held that all traders such as the petitioners situated within the precincts of the Mandi Samiti would have to obtain licences/registration by 4 February 2014.

Facts:

1. The petitioners are registered brokers in the Krishi Utpadan Mandi Samiti, Maudaha, Hamirpur. The petitioners claim to carry out the work of brokers or dalals. According to them, in the ordinary course of business, they arrange contracts for the purchase or sale of agricultural produce on behalf of their principals against the payment of commission

or remuneration, whether in cash or kind as specified under Section 2(b) of the U.P. Krishi Utpadan Mandi Adhiniyam, 1964. On 10/13 December, 2013, the Additional District Magistrate (Finance and Revenue), Hamirpur, passed an order requiring persons in the food business to be registered under the provisions of the Food Safety and Standards Act, 2006. The petitioners submitted their objections on 13 January 2014. By the impugned order dated 16 January 2014, the objections have been rejected and it has been held that all traders such as the petitioners situated within the precincts of the Mandi Samiti would have to obtain licences/registration by 4 February 2014.

Held, while allowing the appeal:

The Food Safety and Standards Act, 2006 was enacted to consolidate the law relating to food and, inter alia, to regulate the manufacture, storage, distribution, sale and import and to ensure availability of safe and wholesome food for human consumption and for matters incidental thereto. Having regard to the underlying object, and principles, Parliament has broadly defined the expressions, 'food', 'food business' and 'ingredients'. In this view of the matter, the order of the District Magistrate requiring registration does not suffer from any error. The petition is, accordingly, dismissed.

CHAPTER NINETEEN

ITC Limited vs. State of Uttarakhand and Ors. (20.05.2015 - UCHC) : MANU/UC/0528/2015

Relative Section:

Food Safety And Standards Act, 2006 - Section 42, Section 52, Section 53

Hon'bleJudges/Coram:

Alok Singh, J.

Equivalent Citation: Writ Petition No. 1119 of 2015 (M/S)

Case Reference: nil

NumberofPagesintheOriginalJudgment: 2

Case Note:

Criminal - Food Safety And Standards Act, 2006-This is a case of mis-branding and misleading advertisement and it is not a case of sub-standard of food or adulteration in the food, therefore, report of Food Analyst is not required.

Facts

Present petition is filed assailing the order dated 20.12.2014, passed by the Designated Officer according sanction to initiate the proceedings under Sections 52 and 53 of the Food Safety and Standards Act, 2006 as well as cognizance/summoning order dated 08.01.2015, passed by Adjudicating Officer/Additional District Magistrate, Hardwar. Under Sections 52 and 53 of the Act, if a person is found guilty for "mis-branding" or "misleading advertisement", penalty may be imposed against such guilty person to the tune which may extend to three lacs and ten lacs respectively. Sections 52 and 53 of the Act do not prescribe any conviction or sentence of jail term.

Held, while allowing the appeal:

1. Since petitioner has put in appearance before the Adjudicating Officer, therefore, As to whether information printed by the petitioner on the level amounts to "mis-branding" or "mis-leading advertisement", can be adjudicated upon by the Adjudicating Officer. Therefore, at this stage, I am not inclined to enter into the controversy to find out as to whether allegation would demonstrate "mis-branding" and "mis-leading advertisement".[5]

2. There seems to be no jurisdictional error in annexure No. 10 and 12 to the writ petition. Writ can be entertained when Writ Court is prima facie satisfied about the jurisdictional error in the impugned orders. Since I do not find any jurisdictional error therein, therefore, I am not inclined to entertain this writ petition. Writ petition is dismissed.[6]

CHAPTER TWENTY

Suraj Mehata vs. State of U.P. (30.04.2019 – ALLHC) : MANU /UP /2188/2019

Relative Section:

Code of Criminal Procedure, 1973 (CrPC) - Section 272; Section 273; Section 439; Constitution Of India - Article 136,Constitution Of India - Article 226, Constitution Of India - Article 32; Food Safety And Standards Act, 2006 - Section 41, Section 42, Section 46 (4), Section 55, Section 57, Sec-68; General Clauses Act 1897 - Section 26; Indian Penal Code 1860, (IPC) - Section 188; Section 272 to Section 276; Section 419; Section 420

Hon'bleJudges/Coram:

Manju Rani Chauhan, J.

Equivalent Citation: 2019(2)ACR1677, 2019 (108) ACC 483

Case Reference:

The State of Maharashtra and Ors. vs. Sayyed Hassan Sayyed Subhan and Ors. MANU/SC/1021/2018; Ramjas Foundation and Anr. vs. Union of India (UOI) and Ors. MANU/SC/0930/2010; Hari Narain vs. Badri Das MANU/SC/0226/1963; Welcom Hotel and Ors. vs. State of Andhra Pradesh and Ors. MANU/SC/0029/1983; G. Narayanaswamy Reddy (dead) by L.Rs. and another vs. Government of Karnataka and another MANU/SC/0386/ 1991; S.P. Chengalvaraya Naidu (dead) by L.Rs. vs. Jagannath (dead) by L.Rs. and others MANU/SC/0192/1994; A.V. Papayya Sastry and Ors. vs. Government of A.P. and Ors. MANU/SC/1214/2007; Prestige Lights Ltd. vs. State Bank of India MANU/SC/3355/2007; Sunil Poddar and Ors. vs. Union Bank of India MANU/SC/0322/2008; K.D. Sharma vs. Steel Authority of India Ltd. and Ors. MANU/SC/3371/2008; G. Jayashree and

Ors. vs. Bhagwandas S. Patel and Ors. MANU/SC/8451/2008; Dalip Singh vs. State of U.P. and Ors. MANU/SC/1886/2009; Alakh Alok Srivastava vs. Union of India (UOI) and Ors. MANU/SC/0489/2018; T.S. Baliah vs. T.S. Rengachari MANU/SC/0238/1968; State of Bihar vs. Murad Ali Khan and Ors. MANU/SC/0470/1988

NumberofPagesintheOriginalJudgment:10

Case Note:

Code of Criminal Procedure, 1973 - Section 439--Indian Penal Code, 1860--Sections 419, 420, 272 and 273--Bail--Allegations in the F.I.R. against the accused persons that they were indulging in manufacture of indigenous liquid butter (deshi ghee) and sesame (teel) oil using adulterated chemical--Persons like applicants engaged in selling adulterated food stuff by mixing toxic chemicals only to earn more money liable to be punished harshly--Adulterated food stuffs made from bones of animals, chemicals, pam oil and soap cream etc. may cause chronic diseases in human beings--No case made out for exercise of discretion in favour of the applicants--Application rejected. [13] to [16]

Facts:

1. It transpires from the record that a first information report has been lodged by the Inspector Shri Mohd. Jainuddin Ansari of Special Task Force, Kanpur Nagar on 11th February, 2019 at 20:30 hrs. against five persons, namely, Suraj Mehata (applicant herein), Sanjay Darwani, Suresh Mishra (applicant herein), Arvind Singh (applicant herein) and Abhishek Kapoor alleging therein that the Police has been informed that in the Sangam Food Factory situate at Govind Pur, with the help of adulterated chemical, indigenous liquid butter (deshi ghee) and sesame (teel) oil were being made, which was causing disjunction on the human body. On the said information, Personnel of Special Task Force came to the factory and saw that R.P.O. chemical were being boiled and packaging was being done by labours with the help of machines. No scent was coming from the boiling chemical, whereas from the packing material, scent of indigenous liquid butter was coming. After mixing adulterated chemicals in the soyabean oil, sesame oil was being made and packaging of the same was done. Since the matter related to food stuff, information was given to the team of F.S.D.A. Kanpur. On the said information, the officers/officials of F.S.D.A. were present including the Food Security Officer, Kanpur. After stopping the packaging work, a joint investigation was initiated. Suraj Mehata (applicant herein), who was partner of the said factory, was interrogated and he told

that Sangam Food Product was a partnership firm and the main partner of the said firm was Sanjay Darwani and other details regarding registration of the said firm and licence of repacker and wholesaler were also disclosed. On seeing the Police, said Sanjay Darwani escaped. Since the notification/ information was found to be correct, Suresh Mishra, Gate Keeper (applicant herein) and Arvind Singh (applicant herein), Supervisor of the said firm were taken into custody. When the accountant, namely, Abhishek Kapoor was searched, it was found that with the owner of the firm, he also escaped taking alongwith him necessary documents. On the pointing out of one of the partners Suraj Mehata (applicant herein), Police Personnel's as well as the officers/officials of Food and Security Department have searched the first floor of firm, where duplicate indigenous liquid butters, duplicate sesame oils, adulterated chemicals, soyabean oil in various quantities as well as wrappers of various brands, printing machine (for printing batch, manufacturing date and printing), turner machine etc. were recovered. On the interrogation, Suraj Mehata told that one liter of chemical (which was found in four drums), when mixed in 220 liters of soyabean oil appeared like sesame oil. By understanding it as sesame oil, people used the same and bought it on the rate of sesame oil.[4]

2. It has been argued by the learned counsel for the applicants that once alleged adulteration is being made in food stuff, then the entire activity of applicants is covered by Special Act i.e., Food Safety and Standard Act, 2006 and the authorities can take action only under the aforesaid Special Act as it postulates an overriding effect over all other food related laws including the F.A. Act and accordingly, invocation of Sections 272 and 273, I.P.C. in matter relating to adulteration is unjustifiable and accordingly, this Court should come to the rescue and reprieve of the applicants. Learned counsels for the applicants has placed reliance upon the Division Bench judgment of the Lucknow Bench of this Court in the case of M/s. Pepsico India Holdings (Pvt.) Ltd. and another v. State of U.P. and others, Writ Petition No. 8254 (MB) of 2010 (decided on 8th September, 2010) alongwith two other connected petitions, wherein it has been laid down that in view of the specific provisions of Food Safety and Standards Act, 2006 (hereinafter referred to as the "F.S.S. Act"), the offences relating to adulteration of food that are governed under the F.S.S. Act after July 29, 2010 are to be treated as per the procedures to be followed for drawing and analysis of samples as have been provided for. The provisions of penalties and prosecution have also been provided therein. Therefore, before launching any prosecution

against an alleged offence of food adulteration, it is necessary for the concerned authorities to follow the mandatory requirements as provided under Sections 41 and 42 of F.S.S. Act and therefore, the Police have no authority or jurisdiction to investigate the matter under F.S.S. Act. It has next been argued by the learned counsel for the applicants that despite time being granted under order of the court dated 1st January, 2019 in Criminal Misc. Bail Application No. 13379 of 2019, no counter-affidavit has been filed on behalf of the State. Non-filing of counter-affidavit will deprive the right to liberty of the applicants. It has next been argued that the period of detention of the applicants of more than two months as on date is excessive, whereas the punishment for the offences punishable under Sections 272 and 273, Cr.P.C. is only for six months along with fine. It has next been argued that the matter relates to food stuff, therefore, the first information report should be lodged by the Food Safety Department and not by the Special Task Force, therefore, in view of the provisions contained in Food Safety and Security Act, 2006, the present first information report is liable to be quashed. It has further been argued that the alleged recovered chemicals were sent for analysis before the Government Public Analysis Laboratory, Lucknow on 11th February, 2019. Out of ten samples, no adulterant was detected in six samples as per the report of the Laboratory, copy of which is on record as Annexure-S.A.-1 to the supplementary affidavit filed in Criminal Misc. Bail Application No. 14478 of 2019. Two samples have been reported to be misbranded and substandard, whereas remaining two samples are reported to be adulterant as per the F.S.S. Act but the same is not injuries to health. Against the said report, the applicants have an efficacious statutory alternative remedy by way of appeal under Section 46 (4)of F.S.S. Act, but because of arrest, they could not avail the said benefit by challenging the said report. It has further been argued that if the said report is found to be correct, then only in that circumstance, the maximum punishment for adulterant is only a penalty not exceeding two lacs. If it is adulterant and injurious to health then also punishment, which can be imposed, is only a penalty not exceeding Rs. Ten lacs as per sub-sections (i) and (ii) of Section 57 of F.S.S. Act.[5]

Held, while allowing the appeal:

1. Having considered the submissions made by the learned counsel for the applicants, the learned A.G.A. for the State and upon perusal of the evidence brought on record as well as the complicity of the applicants but without commenting on the merits of the case, I do not find any good

reason to exercise my discretion in favour of the accused applicants. Thus, all the three bail applications stand rejected.[16]

2. However, the trial court is expected to gear up the trial of the aforesaid case and conclude the same as expeditious, as possible from the date of receipt of certified copy of this order, keeping in view the law laid down by the Apex Court in the case of Alakh Alok Srivastava v. Union of India and another, MANU/SC/0489/2018 : AIR 2018 SC 2004, if there is no legal impediment, in accordance with law, without granting any unnecessary adjournment to either of the parties, provided the applicants fully cooperate in conclusion of the trial, if there is no other legal impediment.[17]

3. Office is directed to transmit a certified copy of this order to the court concerned within a fortnight.[18]

4. It is clarified that any observations, if any, made by this Court are strictly confined to the disposal of the bail application and must not be construed to have any reflection on the ultimate merits of the case.[19]

CHAPTER TWENTY-ONE

Pradeep Kumar Gupta vs. State of U.P. (12.05.2015 – ALLHC) : MANU/UP/0986/2015

Relative Section:

Code of Criminal Procedure, 1973 (CrPC) - Section 195; Section 345; Section 346; Section 446; Constitution Of India - Article 20(2), Article 226, Article 227; Food Safety And Standards Act, 2006 - Section 16, Section 41 to Section 80,Section 97; Indian Penal Code 1860, (IPC) - Section 193; Section 196; Section 228

Hon'bleJudges/Coram:

Pankaj Naqvi, J.

Equivalent Citation: 2015(3)ACR2924, 2015(6)ADJ351, 2015(6) ALJ 426, 2016CriLJ122

Case Reference:

The Chairman, SEBI vs. Shriram Mutual Fund and Anr. MANU/SC/8185/2006; Radheshyam Kejriwal vs. State of West Bengal and Anr. MANU/SC/0134/2011; State of Uttar Pradesh and Ors. vs. Mukhtar Singh and Ors. MANU/UP/0156/1957; Maqbool Hussain vs. The State of Bombay MANU/SC/0062/1953; S.A.L. Narayan Row and Anr. vs. Ishwarlal Bhagwandas and Anr. MANU/SC/0160/1965; M/s. Nagpur Cable Operators' Association vs. Commissioner of Police, Nagpur and another MANU/MH/0035/1996

NumberofPagesintheOriginalJudgment:9

Case Note:

Food Adulteration- Criminal - This appeal styled as "Criminal Appeal" is preferred under Section 71(6) of the Food Safety and Standards Act, 2006 (in short 'the Act'), assailing the order dated 17.3.2015 in Criminal Appeal No. 19 of 2015 passed by District Judge, Agra, whereby the order of the Adjudicating Officer dated 19.2.2015 imposing a penalty of Rs. 5 lacs stands reduced to 50%, as a pre conditional deposit for admission of the appeal.

The core issue which falls for consideration is as to the nature of adjudication proceedings contemplated under Chapter X of the Act i.e., whether such proceedings are civil or criminal in nature as an answer on the said issue would have a bearing on the cognoscibility of this appeal before this bench on the criminal side of the jurisdiction.

Facts:

The appellant claims to be a petty food vendor engaged in the business under the Act; on 9.11.2012 the Food Safety Officer inspected his shop, purchased a sample of paneer, which as per report of public analyst was found to contain fats less than the prescribed limit of 50% hence, sample was found to be sub-standard. On the basis of the report and after requisite sanction from the Designated Officer under the Act, a complaint dated 10.11.2012 was filed by the Food Safety Officer before the Adjudicating Officer/Additional District Magistrate. The Adjudicating Officer after notice and hearing the appellant passed an order dated 19.2.2015 imposing a penalty of Rs. 5 lacs. The appellant preferred an appeal under Section 70(1) before the Food Safety Appellate Tribunal (FSAT) i.e. the District Judge, Agra The F.S.A.T., vide its order dated 17.3.2015 passed a conditional order that the appeal be admitted subject to deposit of 50% of the penalty, which is impugned herein.

Held, while allowing the appeal:

In view of aforesaid discussion, the Court is of the view that both the Adjudicating Officer and the Food Safety Appellate Tribunal, while adjudging the quantum of penalty under Chapter X of the Act of 2006 were only exercising the powers of the Civil Court as their determination was only confined to the adjudication on the quantum of penalty and nothing else. They had no jurisdiction or power or authority to impose any punishment/sentence, which power was only conferred upon the Special Courts or the Ordinary Criminal Courts as the case may be, for prosecution of an offence under the Act. If this is the position, which is emerging from the analysis of Sections 68, 70 and 71 of the Act, then the Court has no option but to hold that an appeal against an order of the Adjudicating

Officer under Section 70(1) before the Food Safety Appellate Tribunal could not be filed as criminal appeal and would only lie as a civil miscellaneous appeal. Similarly, the appeal provided under sub-section (6) of Section 71 of the Act of 2006 against any decision or order of the Tribunal would lie to the High Court not as criminal appeal but as an appeal from order on the civil side. The objection of learned A.G.A. is upheld. It is accordingly directed that:

(i) An appeal under Section 70(1) of the Food Safety and Standards Act, 2006 against the decision of the Adjudicating Officer under Section 68 before the Food Safety Appellate Tribunal would be treated as "Civil Miscellaneous Appeal" and not as "Criminal Appeal".

(ii) The appeals filed under Section 71(6) of the Food Safety and Standards Act, 2006 before this Court be treated as an appeal from order and shall be dealt with on the civil side accordingly. The instant appeal shall therefore be de-registered as criminal appeal and it be re-registered as an appeal from order. Registry to take follow up action.

(iii) The Registrar General is directed to circulate a copy of this judgment to the subordinate judgeships.

Learned counsel for appellant is permitted to make necessary corrections in the memorandum of appeal. Interim order granted earlier would continue till the next date.

It is made clear that the Court has not adjudicated the issue on merits and the observations made hereinabove were only confined to determine the cognoscibility of this appeal before this Bench (Criminal).

This appeal shall be placed before the appropriate Bench as fresh on 20.7.2015 but subject to the convenience of the bench.

The Court places on record its appreciation for the valuable assistance rendered by Sri Rajiv Lochan Sukla, as Amicus Curiae in this case.

Adv. Jayprakash Somani's Videos On Law

Adv. Jayprakash Somani's Videos on Law on Youtube- 'jaysomani64' channel

1) SLP in Supreme Court / Special Leave Petitions in the Supreme Court of India

2) Transfer of Civil & Criminal Cases by the Supreme Court of India / Transfer of Matrimonial Cases

3) Appellate Jurisdiction of the Supreme Court of India

4) Jurisdictions of the Supreme Court of India

5) Public Interest Litigation in the Supreme Court of India / PIL in Supreme Court

6) Article 32 Writ Petitions in the Supreme Court of India

7) Bail Matters Top 10 Supreme Court Cases

8) FIR Quashing in High Court & Supreme Court

9) Bail & Anticipatory Bail Matters in Supreme Court

10) Insolvency & Bankruptcy Matters in the Supreme Court

11) Insolvency & Bankruptcy Code 2016 Part 1

12) Insolvency & Bankruptcy Code 2016 Part 2

13) Insolvency & Bankruptcy Code 2016 Part 3

14) Corporate Liquidation Process

15) Supreme Court Rules & Procedures Webinar of 2.5 hour on Zoom

16) RDDBFI Act, 1993 (Introduction)

17) The Indian Contact Act 1872

18) Negotiable Instruments Act (Introduction)

19) How to avoid matrimonial disputes& some more videos

20) SEBI Matters in the Supreme Court

21) Matrimonial Matters: Supreme Court's 20 Case Laws

22) Consumer Matters Supreme Court's 20 Case Laws

23) Service Matters Supreme Court's 20 Case Laws

24) How to Search Lawyer for Your Matter

25) Property Matters Supreme Court's 20 Case Laws

26) Bail Matters: Supreme Court's 20 Case Laws

27) Supreme Court / High Court Vacation Benches

28) 69000 Teacher's Recruitment Matters of UP Government in the Supreme Court

29) Contempt of Court Matters in the Supreme Court

30) Advocate Act's Matters in the Supreme Court

31) Business Law Matters in the Supreme Court

32) Banking Matters in the Supreme Court

33) Labour Law Matters in the Supreme Court

34) Arbitration Matters in the Supreme Court

35) Careers in Law -Zoom Webinar by Adv. Jayprakash Somani

36) Civil Matters in the Supreme Court

37) Consumer Protection Act | Consumer Matters in the Supreme Court

38) Corporate Matters in the Supreme Court

39) Criminal Matters in the Supreme Court

40) Role of Respondent in the Supreme Court of India

41) Motor Vehicle Accident Matters in Supreme Court with case laws

42) Article 131 Original Suits in Supreme Court

43) PIL in Supreme Court/ Public Interest Litigations in the Supreme Court of India'

44) CAB Citizenship Amendment Bill is not Unconstitutional

45) Supreme Court of India Cases & Process – Marathi

46) Legal Services Export / Export of Legal Services

47) Transfer of Matrimonial Cases by the Supreme Court of India

48) Public Interest Litigation PIL

49) The Specific Relief Act (Introduction)

50) Corporate Insolvency Resolution Process CIRP

51) ABMM's Career 5 - Careers in Law

52) Transfer of cases by Supreme Court

53) Writ Petitions in High Court & Supreme Court of India

54) Supreme Court Jurisdictions - Appeals, SLP, Writ Petitions, Transfer, Original, Review, Curative

55) LEGAL INDIA TV Show: Cases Handled in Supreme Court

56) Corporate Liquidation Process

57) Legal Services Export / Export of Legal Services

58) Corporate Laws

59) Election Matters- Supreme Court's 20 Case Laws

60) Companies Act, 2013

62) Competition Act, 2002

63) Banking Matters - Supreme Court's 20 Case Laws

64) Election Matters in the Supreme Court

65) Armed Forces Tribunal Matters in the Supreme Court

66) Compassionate Appointment Service matter

67) Foreign Exchange Management Act FEMA

68) Foreign Trade Policy 2021-26 Proposed

69) Customs Act 1962

70) Narcotic Drugs and Psychotropic Substances Act, 1985 NDPS Act

71) Foreign Trade Development & Regulation Act, 1992

72) How to Search Good Advocate in the Supreme Court of India

73) Sr. Adv Vikas Singh's Interview in Nani Palkhivala Wednesday Law Club

74) Indian Penal Code (I. P. C.)

75) Criminal Procedure Code (Cr. P. C.)

76) Commercial Courts & International Arbitration - by Mr. Jaideep Gupta, Senior Advocate in Nani Palkhivala Wednesday Law Club

77) Sr. Adv Ranji Thomos in Nani Palkhivala Wednesday Law Club

78) Urgent Matters in Supreme Court during vacations

79) 498A Bail Matters in Supreme Court

81) 376 Bail Matters in Supreme Court

82) 302, 304, 307, 308 Bail Matters in Supreme Court

83) 138, 420 Bail Matters in Supreme Court

84) POCSO Act Bail Matters in Supreme Court

85) NDPS Act Bail Matters in Supreme Court

86) What is ED (Enforcement Directorate)?

87) Prevention of Money Laundering Act, 2002 (PMLA Act)

88) Insolvency & Bankruptcy Code- Supreme Court Case Laws. Webinar in Nani Palkhivala Wednesday Law Club

89) What is NCLT & NCLAT?

90) Acquittal from 376- Supreme Court's some case laws in Nani Palkhivala Wednesday Law Club dt 28.7.22

91) Insolvency & Bankruptcy in India

92) Can we file case directly in the Supreme Court?

93) Adv. Anuja Pethia has cleared AOR Exam 2021 with 77% marks - Her interview in Nani Palkhivala Wednesday Law Club

94) Customs Act - Supreme Court Case Laws & Interview of AOR Adv. Anuja Pethia in Nani Palkhivala Law Club.

95) The Uttar Pradesh Public Service Tribunals Act, 1976

96) POCSO Act - Supreme Court Case Laws & Interview of AOR Adv. Shoumendu Mukharji & Adv. Nishant Verma in Nani Palkhivala Law Club.

97) Who Can Trigger CIRP Process Under Insolvency Law of India

98) The Uttar Pradesh Government Servant Discipline and Appeal Rules, 1999

99) CIRP Application Under Sec 7 by FC

100) Information Technology Act 2000

101) Uttar Pradesh Recruitment of Dependants of Government Servants Dying in Harness Rules, 1974

102) Foreign Exchange Management Act 1999 & Supreme Court's Case Laws on FEMA & Leading Case of AOR Exam in Nani Palkhivala Law Club.

103) Arbitration and Conciliation Act 1996 & It's Supreme Court Case Laws in Nani Palkhivala Wednesday Law Club.

104) Narcotic Drugs & Psychotropic Substances Act 1985 (NDPS Act) & It's Supreme Court Case Laws in Nani Palkhivala Wednesday Law Club.

105) Recovery of Debts and Bankruptcy Act 1993

106) Uttar Pradesh Land Revenue Code 2006

107) CIRP Application Under Sec 9 by OC

108) CIRP Application Under Sec 10 by CD

109) Hindu Succession Act, 1956

110) Maharashtra Civil Services Rules, 1981

111) Indian Contract Act, 1872 & Supreme Court's Case Laws" in Nani Palkhiwala Wednesday Law Club

112) Securities and Exchange Board of India Act, 1992 i. e. SEBI Act 1992 & Case Laws on Insiders Trading" in Nani Palkhiwala Wednesday Law Club

113) Moratorium Under Section 14 of IBC, 2016

114) Hindu Marriage Act, 1955

115) Maharashtra Land Revenue Code, 1966

116) 64 Leading Cases of AOR Exam Session 1 :- Cases 1 to16 in Nani Palkhiwala Wednesday Law Club

117) 64 Leading Cases of AOR Exam Session 2: Cases 17 to 32 in Nani Palkhivala Wednesday Law Club

118) 64 Leading Cases of AOR Examination Session 3: Cases 33 to 48 in Nani Palkhivala Wednesday Law Club

119) 64 Leading Cases of AOR Exam Session 4: Cases 49 to 64 in Nani Palkhivala Wednesday Law Club

120) Labour Laws of India: Part 1 - 4 New Labour Law Codes of India

121) New Labour Laws Part 2 The Code on Wages, 2019

122) New Labour Laws Part 3:- The Code on Social Security, 2020

123) Argue in English Fluently & Confidently - Two months online course.

124) SLP Admission in the Supreme Court. 2023 (Hindi)

125) Transfer of Petitions from the Supreme Court (Hindi)

126) Review Petition in the Supreme Court.(Hindi)

127) Recovery of debts from the Company (Hindi)

128) How to search 'Good Insolvency & Bankruptcy Consultant?' (HINDI)

129) Curative Petition in the Supreme Court

130) AFT Appeals in the Supreme Court (HINDI)

131) NCLAT's Appeals in the Supreme Court.

132) Transfer Petition: Which matters can we transfer?

133) SLP Types of SLP in the Supreme court of India (English).

134) Argue in English Fluently and Confidently in the High Court & Supreme Court'.

List Of Adv. Jayprakash Somani's Books

List of Adv. Jayprakash Somani's Published Books

1. Supreme Court of India's Leading Case Laws on 'Insolvency & Bankruptcy Code 2016'

2. Bail Matters – Supreme Court's Latest Leading Case Laws

3. Arbitration Matters- Supreme Court's Latest Leading Case Laws

4. Property Matters - Supreme Court's Latest Leading Case Laws

5. Matrimonial Matters- Supreme Court's Latest Leading Case Laws

6. Election Matters- Supreme Court's Latest Leading Case Laws

7.SEBI Matters- Supreme Court's Latest Leading Case Laws

8. Banking Matters- Supreme Court's Latest Leading Case Laws

9. Service Matters- Supreme Court's Latest Leading Case Laws

10. Contempt of Court Matters- Supreme Court's Latest Leading Case Laws

11. Consumer Protection Matters- Supreme Court's Latest Leading Case Laws

12. Corporate Law- Supreme Court's Latest Leading Case Laws

13. Supreme Court's AOR Exam- Leading Cases

14. Armed Force Tribunal - Supreme Court's Latest Leading Case Laws

15. Acquittal From 376 - Supreme Court's Latest Leading Case Laws

16. Negotiable instrument – Supreme Court's Latest Leading Case Laws

17. Contract Act- Supreme Court's Latest Leading Case Laws

18. Insider trading- Supreme Court's Latest Leading Case Laws

19. Foreign Exchange and Management Act- Supreme Court's Latest Leading Case Laws

20. Income Tax Act- Supreme Court's Latest Leading Case Laws

21. Company Law- Supreme Court's Latest Leading Case Laws

22. Competition & Monopoly Matters- Supreme Court's Latest Leading Case Laws

23. Compassionate Appointment- Service Matters- Supreme Court's Latest Leading Case Laws

24. Compulsory Retirement- Service Matters- Supreme Court's Latest Leading Case Laws

25. Voluntary Retirement- Service Matters- Supreme Court's Latest Leading Case Laws

26. Removal/Dismissal/Termination from Service- Supreme Court's Latest Leading Case Laws

27. Seniority- Service Matter- Supreme Court's Latest Leading Case Laws

28. Promotion- Service Matter- Supreme Court's Latest Leading Case Laws

29. Equal Pay for Equal Work- Service Matter- Supreme Court's Latest Leading Case Laws

30. Condition of Service- Service Matter- Supreme Court's Latest Leading Case Laws

31. Customs Act- Supreme Court's Leading Case Laws

32. Information Technology Act- Supreme Court's Leading Case Laws

33. SEC. 125 CR. P. C.- Supreme Court's Leading Case Laws

34. SEC. 498A OF I. P. C.- Supreme Court's Leading Case Laws

35. MOTOR VEHICLE ACT- Supreme Court's Leading Case Laws

36. CONDITION OF SERVICE- SERVICE MATTER- Supreme Court's Leading Case Laws

37. SUSPENSION- SERVICE MATTER- Supreme Court's Leading Case Laws

38. Reservation in SC, ST, OBC- Service Matter- Supreme Court's Leading Case Laws

39. NARCOTIC DRUGS AND PSYCHOTROPIC SUBSTANCES (NDPS) ACT - Supreme Court of India's Latest Leading Case Laws

40. SEC 302 IPC - Supreme Court of India's Latest Leading Case Laws

41. PROTECTION OF CHILDREN FROM SEXUAL OFFENCES ACT (POCSO) - Supreme Court of India's Latest Leading Case Laws

42. PMLA ACT BAIL MATTERS - Supreme Court of India's Leading Case Laws

43. SEC 376 BAIL MATTERS - Supreme Court of India's Leading Case Laws

44. SEC 302 BAIL MATTERS - Supreme Court of India's Leading Case Laws

45. POCSO ACT BAIL MATTERS - Supreme Court of India's Leading Case Laws

46. JUVENILE JUSTICE ACT- Supreme Court of India's Leading Case Laws

47. TRANSFER OF PROPERTY ACT- Supreme Court of India's Leading Case Laws

48. PROFESSIONAL ETHICS OF ADVOCATES- AOR EXAM- SUPREME COURT'S LEADING CASE LAWS

49. WHITE COLLAR CRIME- SUPREME COURT'S LEADING CASE LAWS

50. SEC 302 BAIL MATTERS- SUPREME COURT'S LEADING CASE LAWS

51. SEC 7 IBC 2016 - SUPREME COURT'S LATEST LEADING CASE LAW

52. ADVERSE POSSESSION IN PROPERTY MATTER - SUPREME COURT'S LATEST LEADING CASE LAWS

53. ARMED FORCE TRIBUNAL ACT- SUPREME COURT'S LATEST LEADING CASE LAWs

54. ESSENTIAL COMMODITIES ACT 1955- SUPREME COURT'S LATEST LEADING CASE LAWS

Books are available online in India

1. Notion Press: https://notionpress.com/author/jayprakash_somani

2. Amazon: https://www.amazon.in/s?k=jayprakash+somani

3. Flipkart: https://www.flipkart.com/search?q=Jayprakash%20Somani

Books are available online at International Market

4. Amazon International: https://www.amazon.com/s?k=jayprakash+somani

5. Amazon United Kingdom: https://www.amazon.co.uk/s?k=jayprakash+somani

6. E-Books/Kindle edition at National & International Level: https://www.amazon.in/s?k=jaypraksh+somani

Adv Jayprakash Somani's Online Courses

Download our app to get access to our Free Videos, Free Bare Acts, Free Study Material in Legal as well as International Business Regime.

Android App Link ;-https://clpandrea.page.link/cmSm

Ios APp Link :-https://apps.apple.com/us/app/classplus/id1324522260

Login with org code ;- (qywzji)

Web Link ;-https://qywzji.courses.store/

Download App on Google play store - Type

Jayprakash Somani SupremeCourt

Enter Caption

Legal Courses :

1. SLP- Bail Matters- Drafting & Successful Arguing in the Supreme Court.

Description -This Course is helpful to Advocates, Litigants, Law Officers, Law Students, Law Schools, Individual. Course contains 8 Videos + Study Material+ PDF Books. Access to this course is for Two Years. Expected duration of this course is one month only.

Topics : 1. SLP- Bail Matters- Drafting & Successful Arguing in the Supreme Court, **2.** Types of bails, **3.** Laws related to bail matters, **4.** How to read Impugned Order of High Court & frame substantial question of laws, **5.** How to draft excellent SLP,**6.** Searching of citations/ case laws, **7.** How to argue in admission hearings, **8.** How argue in after notice hearing.

Speaker: Jayprakash Bansilal Somani, MBA (Foreign Trade), LL. B. Advocate, Supreme Court of India & IP www.jayprakashsomani.com Call: P. A. 9322188701

2. SLP- Succession Matters- Drafting & Successful Arguing in the Supreme Court.

Description - This Course is helpful to Advocates, Litigants, Law Officers, Law Students, Law Schools, Individual. Course contains 9 Videos + Study Material+ PDF Books. Access to this course is for Two Years. Expected duration of this course is one month only.

Topics :1. SLP- Succession Matters- Drafting & Successful Arguing in the Supreme Court,**2.** Information about Succession Matters,**3.** Laws related to Succession Matters, **4.** How to read Impugned Order of High Court to frame substantial questions of law, **5.** How to draft excellent synopsis & list of date, **6.** Drafting of SLP of Succession Matter, **7.** Searching of citations/ case laws, **8.** How to prepare notes & then argue in admission hearings, **9.** How to prepare notes & then argue in after notice final hearing.

Speaker: Jayprakash Bansilal Somani, MBA (Foreign Trade), LL. B. Advocate, Supreme Court of India & IP www.jayprakashsomani.com Call: P. A. 9322188701

3. Legal Vocabulary & its practice pattern to Argue in High Court and Supreme Court / Improve Your Legal English

Description - This Course is helpful to Advocates, Litigants, Law Officers, Law Students, Law Schools, Individual. Course contains 11 Videos + Study Material+ PDF Books. Access to this course is for Two Years. Expected duration of this course is three month only.

Topics : **1.** Legal Vocabulary & its practice pattern to Argue in High Court and Supreme Court / Improve Your Legal English, **2.** 1000 legal verbs with its three forms, **3.** Twelve Tenses with its running practice, **4.** One Pdf book on legal vocabulary & its practice pattern with Latin Terms, **5.** Second Pdf book on legal vocabulary & its practice pattern with Latin Terms, **6.** Some Videos of CJI Dr. Dhananjay Chandrachud for the practice of good legal English, **7.** Some Video/Audio Lectures of Legend Nani Palkhivala for standard perfect legal English & flow of Speech, **8.** Some Videos of renowned Sr. Advocates from Mumbai for flow, legal vocabulary & their struggle in legal journey, **9.** Some Videos of Sr. Advocates of the Supreme Court for flow & legal vocabulary,**10.** Some Videos of foreign persons to improve Professional English & thinking process in English,**11.** Some important legal doctrines with case laws.

Speaker: Jayprakash Bansilal Somani, MBA (Foreign Trade), LL. B. Advocate, Supreme Court of India & IP www.jayprakashsomani.com Call: P. A. 9322188701.

4. SLP- Property Matters - Drafting and Successful Arguing in the Supreme Court.

Description - This Course is helpful to Advocates, Litigants, Law Officers, Law Students, Law Schools 8 Individual. Course contains 9 Videos + Study Material+ PDF Books. Access to this course is for Two Years. Expected duration of this course is one month only.

Topics : 1. SLP- Property Matters - Drafting and Successful Arguing in the Supreme Court, **2.** Types of Property Matters, **3.** Laws related to Property Matters, **4.** How to read Impugned Order of High Court to guide client & frame substantial question of laws, **5.** How to draft Synopsis & List of Dates in Property Matter, **6.** How to draft excellent SLP of Property Matter, **7.** Searching of citations/ case laws with specific paras, **8.** How to argue confidently in admission hearings, **9.** How argue confidently in after notice & final hearings.

Speaker: Jayprakash Bansilal Somani, MBA (Foreign Trade), LL. B. Advocate, Supreme Court of India & IP www.jayprakashsomani.com Call: P. A. 9322188701.

International Business Courses -
1. Agri Products Exports - Scope from India.

Description - This Course is helpful to Agriculturalists, Entrepreneurs, Exporters, Importers, Students. Course contains 12 Videos + Study Material+ PDF Books. Access to this course is for Two Years. Expected duration of this course is one month only.

Topics : **1-** Agri Products Exports - Scope from India,**2.** Agri Export's share in India's total export, **3.** Agri Export Promotional Council's Support, **4.** Top 10 Agri export countries, **5.** Top 10 Agri export product, **6.** India's share in World's Agri Exports, **7.** Onion Exports from India, **8.** Rice Exports from India, **9.** Mango Exports from India, **10.** Fresh Vegetable Exports, **11.** Fresh Fruits Exports, **12.** Export of Agri Allied Products.

Speaker: Jayprakash Bansilal Somani, MBA (Foreign Trade), LL. B. Advocate, Supreme Court of India & IP www.jayprakashsomani.com Call: P. A. 9322188701.

2. Textile Exports - Scope from India.

Description -This Course is helpful to Textile Business Houses, Entrepreneurs, Exporters, Importers, Students. Course contains 14 Videos

+ Study Material+ PDF Books. Access to this course is for Two Years. Expected duration of this course is one month only.

Topics :1- Textile Exports - Scope from India, **2**. Textile Export's share in India's total exports, **3**. Support of Textile Export Promotional Council, **4**. Top 10 Countries in Textile Exports, **5**. Top 10 Products in Textile Exports, **6**. Export of Readymade Garments, **7**. Export of Man-made Textiles, **8**. Export of Handloom Products, **9**. Export of Wool & Woollen Textiles, **10**. Export of Silk, **11**. Exports of Handicrafts & Carpets, **12**. Exports of Coir & Coir Manufacturers, **13**. Exports of Jute,14. India's share in World's total textile expor.

Speaker: Jayprakash Bansilal Somani, MBA (Foreign Trade), LL. B. Advocate, Supreme Court of India & IP www.jayprakashsomani.com Call: P. A. 9322188701.

3. Export Import Procedure - Perfect Documentation & It's Management.

Description -This Course is helpful to Business Men, Service Providers, Entrepreneurs, Exporters, Importers, Students. Course contains 13 Videos + Study Material+ PDF Books. Access to this course is for Two Years. Expected duration of this course is three months only.

Topics : **1**. Export Import Procedure, Perfect Documentation & Its management, **2**. Company Formation, **3**. Opening of Bank Account in AD Bank, **4**. Export Procedure points, **5**. Import Procedure Points, **6**. Taking Import Export Code, **7**. Taking RCMC number,**8**. Registration at Port when necessary, **9**. Quality Inspection Certificate of Goods, **10**. CHA & its roll, **11**. Custom Formalities, **12**. Export Documents such as Invoice, Bill of Lading, Insurance Certificate, Quality Inspection Certificate & others, **13**. Excellent Management of Export & Imports Documents.

Speaker: Jayprakash Bansilal Somani, MBA (Foreign Trade), LL. B. Advocate, Supreme Court of India & IP www.jayprakashsomani.com Call: P. A. 9322188701.

4. Jewellery Exports - Scope from India, Expected

Description - You can understand world wide scope for Jems & Jewellery in multidimensional ways. 14 videos of this course will create positive spark among you to enter into the Exports & Imports of Gems & Jewellery and other products. Chance to ask your query to Somani Sir every week.

Topics :1. Jewellery Exports - Scope from India, **2**. Jewellery Export's share in India's total exports, **3**. Support of Jems & Jewellery Export

Promotional Council, **4.** Top 10 Countries in Jewellery Exports, **5.** Top 10 Products in Jewellery Exports, **6.** Export of Cut & Polished Diamonds, **7.** Export of Gold Jewellery, **8.** Export of Plain Gold Jewellery, **9.** Export of Studded Gold Jewellery, **10.** Export of Silver Jewellery, **11.** Exports of Platinum Jewellery, **12.** Exports of Imitation Jewellery, **13.** Exports of Articles of Gold, Silver & others,**14.** India's share in World's total Jewellery export.

Speaker: Jayprakash Bansilal Somani, MBA (Foreign Trade), LL. B. Advocate, Supreme Court of India & IP www.jayprakashsomani.com Call: P. A. 9322188701.

5. Export Import Finance Management with LC, ECGC & Venture Capital.

Description -You can understand A to Z about International Finance with LC, ECGC & Venture Capital in simple language & with illustrations. 11 videos of this course will create positive spark among you regarding International Finance Management with practical tips. Chance to ask your query to Somani Sir every week.

Topics : **1.** Export Import Finance Management with LC, ECGC & Venture Capital, **2.** Which is good & excellent source of finance, **3.** Banking Finance, **4.** List of Banks which provides finance for International Business, **5.** How to start business in Less or Zero Capital, **6.** Letter of Credit, **7.** Types of LCs **8.** Scrutiny of L/C, **9.** ECGC Policy, **10.** Venture Capital Finance., **11.** Ideal formula of Investment & continues growth.

Speaker: Jayprakash Bansilal Somani, MBA (Foreign Trade), LL. B. Advocate, Supreme Court of India & IP www.jayprakashsomani.com Call: P. A. 9322188701.

6. Shipping & Logistics in International Business with live links of Ports, ICDs, CHAs etc.

Description -This Course is helpful to any Businessman, Professionals, Entrepreneurs, Exporters, Importers, CHAs, & Students. Course contains following 10 Videos + Study Material+ PDF Books. Access to this course is for Two Years. Expected duration of this course is three months only.

Topics : **1.** Shipping & Logistics in International Business with live links of Ports, ICDs, CHAs etc, **2.** Roll of CHA in Shipping & Logistics of International Business, **3.** How to find good & genuine CHA, **4.** Courier/ post service for small parcel, **5.** India's important Ports & ICDs with live links, **6.** How & what to study Ports/ ICDs websites, **7.** Art to reduce charges of Shipping & logistics, **8.** Information about some Top International Ports with live links, **9.** Roll of Customs in Exports & Imports,**10.** How to become CHA .

Speaker: Jayprakash Bansilal Somani, MBA (Foreign Trade), LL. B. Advocate, Supreme Court of India & IP www.jayprakashsomani.com Call: P. A. 9322188701.

7. International Business Marketing Part 1: Finding Potential & Genuine Buyers for Exports and Suppliers for Imports.

Description -You can understand Seven Excellent ways to Find Potential & Genuine Buyers for Exports and Suppliers for Imports with illustrations. 11 videos of this course will create positive spark among you regarding International Business Marketing with practical tips. Chance to ask your query to Somani Sir every week.

Topics : 1. International Business Marketing Part 1: Finding Potential & Genuine Buyers for Exports and Suppliers for Imports,**2.** Seven Excellent Ways to find Potential Buyers for Exports, **3.** Top 20 B to B Websites in the World, **4.** Searching Potential Buyers from B to B Sites. Is this safe & good way to search potential buyers, **5.** Searching Potential Buyers through Export Promotional Councils & Its Magazines, **6.** Searching Potential Buyers with help from Embassies, **7.** Searching Potential Buyers through Chamber of Commerce at global level, **8.** Searching Potential Buyers from International Trade Fairs & Exhibitions, **9.** Searching Potential Buyers through your friends & relatives or any Indian Person in focus countries, **10.** How to find focus countries for your products or services, **11.** Taking references from establish buyer/seller.

Speaker: Jayprakash Bansilal Somani, MBA (Foreign Trade), LL. B. Advocate, Supreme Court of India & IP www.jayprakashsomani.com Call: P. A. 9322188701.

8.International Business Marketing Part 2: Communication Skill to take repeated orders from Potential Buyers

Description - You can learn Perfect Communication Skills to initiate International Trade with foreign buyers and art to take repeated orders from these Potential Buyers with illustrations. 11 videos of this course will create positive spark among you to reach upto One Star Exporter Level rapidly and subsequent journey to reach upto Five Star Export House. Chance to ask your query to Somani Sir every week.

Topics :1. International Business Marketing Part 2: Communication Skill to take repeated orders from Potential Buyers,**2.** Preparation of Impressive Company Profile, **3.** Excellent Product CatLog for International

Market, **4.** Phone Calls with maintaining dignity of ourself & our country, **5.** Sending emails, **6.** Sending what's app messages, **7.** Technique of repeated follow up, **8.** Art of taking 100% advance payments, **9.** Before giving credit facility how to look credibility of potential buyers or suppliers, **10.** Art of earning good profit of margin, **11.** Art of managing international clients.

Speaker: Jayprakash Bansilal Somani, MBA (Foreign Trade), LL. B. Advocate, Supreme Court of India & IP www.jayprakashsomani.com Call: P. A. 9322188701.